MOUNTAIN B

A Guide to Singletrack Trails in The Buckeye State
Second Edition

James Buratti

What the press said...

Mountain Biking Ohio "ends the 'searching' by hardcore off-roaders" with what is "easily considered one of the most comprehensive mountain biking guide books in the Midwest."

-Bike Magazine, (Nov/Dec 1997, Vol 4, No. 10)

"(T)his book is destined to become the Buckeye Bikers' Bible."

--Todd Williams, North Coast Sports Book Review

What you said...

"To get your riding fix, you must have this book."

--Doug

"Mt. Biking Ohio is the bomb...That book has changed my life, I am suprised it is not a best seller!"

--Ed

"Great job!!! I can't wait to ride some of these trails."

--Jose

Acknowledgments

The author wishes to thank his many friends who helped to make this book possible. Either on the trail or at a computer, it would not have happened without you all. Big thanks to the COMBO weekend warriors Doug, Michael, and Andree. I also want to thank everyone who enjoyed the first edition and took the time to let me know. I hope you find this one just as humorous and helpful. Extra special thanks to Mary Hoffelt. Thanks to Sumati Ganeshan who made the first edition so legible. The second edition owes much to Chris Thomas, a friend skilled at both words and wheels. Lastly, I must thank my chief investors for this book and my life - my mom and dad. Thanks again and happy trails.

Copyright © 1999 by James Buratti

First Edition 1997

Second Edition 1999

All rights reserved including the right of reproduction in whole or in any part in any form, including all maps.

All photographs Copyright © James Buratti. Some photos provided by David Diller.

Cover photo: Rudy Sroka of Team Burn racing at Vulture's Knob Race Course, Wooster, Ohio.

Cover design, Single-Track Surfer, and layout assistance by Mary Hoffelt.

IMBA "Rules of the Trail" printed with permission.

Published by Single Track Press, Columbus, Ohio
ISBN 0-9657566-1-0

Single Track Press Website http://www.single-track.com
Questions, comments, praise, scorn or a cool trail you want to include? E-mail us at mbo@single-track.com

Text printed on tree-free, chlorine-free bamboo pulp paper with soy-based inks. Cover contains on 50% recycled fiber with 20% post-consumer fiber.

Disclaimer: This information is provided for personal use only. Mountain biking is an inherently dangerous sport. James Buratti and Single Track Press take no responsibility for any injuries, either physical or mental, suffered while using any of this information. If you're smart you'll stick to reading or surfin' the web and stay off that dangerous, two-wheeled beast lurking in the corner.

MOUNTAIN BIKING OHIO

A Guide to Singletrack Trails in The Buckeye State
Second Edition

James Buratti

Single Track Press

Table of Contents

Map of Ohio's Trails

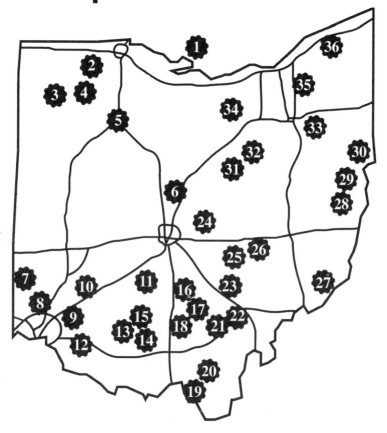

Taking a break at Cementary Hill, Scioto Trail State Forest.

List of Ohio's Trails

Trail #	Trail Name	Trail Miles	Trail Rating	Page #
1	Kelly's Island	5	Easy	16
2	Maumee	5	Easy	18
3	Oakwood Park	3.5	Easy	20
4	Mary Jane Thurston	6	Easy	22
5	Handlebar Hollow	2	Easy	24
6	Alum Creek	7	Easy-Mod	26
7	Hueston Woods	10	Easy-Mod	28
8	Harbin Park	5	Easy-Mod	30
9	Landen-Deerfield	3.5	Easy	31
10	Caesar Creek	13	Easy-Mod	32
11	Deer Creek	1.2	Easy	34
12	East Fork	4.4	Easy-Mod	36
13	Rocky Fork	2	Mod	38
14	Pike	15	Chal	40
15	Paint Creek	14	Easy-Mod	42
16	Great Seal	20	Mod-Chal	44
17	Tar Hollow	2.6	Easy-Mod	46
18	Scioto Trail	40	Easy-Mod-Chal	48
19	Hanging Rock	26	Chal	52
20	Pine Creek	20	Chal	54
21	Richland Furnace	7	Mod-Chal	56
22	Lake Hope	3	Easy-Mod	58
23	Monday Creek	72	Chal	60
24	Denison University	4	Easy	64
25	Perry	13	Mod-Chal	66
26	Zanesville Velo-Z	5	Mod-Chal	68
27	Marietta Unit	82	Chal	70
28	Mickey's Mountain	15	Mod-Chal	74
29	Jefferson Lake	22	Mod	76
30	Beaver Creek	8	Mod-Chal	78
31	Mohican Wilderness	3	Mod-Chal	80
32	Vulture's Knob	7	Mod-Chal	81
33	Quail Hollow	2	Easy	84
34	Fildley	2	Easy	86
35	Alpine Valley	3	Mod	88
36	Atchinson	3	Mod	89

Introduction To The Second Edition

Welcome back! Or if you're new to the ride, welcome along! Mountain Biking Ohio is growing by leaps and bounds as you may have noticed from the 19 new places to ride included in this book. Yep, we're up to 36 different trail systems located in almost every corner of Ohio. And the amount of trail has increased to 456 miles, up from 270 just two years ago. That's the good news.

Now a little bad news. None of Ohio's major metropolitan areas have opened a single mile of trail to mountain bikes. Cleveland, Cincinnati, Columbus. Zero, zip, nada. And this is where most riders live. On the flip side, Ohio's small towns have taken the lead in providing for their citizens needs. Napoleon, Findlay, Fairfield. Trails, trails, trails. Small town living is the life for me.

Also in need of a big push in the right direction is the Ohio State Division of Forestry which hasn't opened any new trails to mountain bikes since making the trails in Scioto Trail State Forest multiuse years ago. Mohican, Tar Hollow, and Shawnee are examples of state forests which would make ideal mountain biking destinations. Ohio's Division of Parks and Recreation is getting with the program, with more parks opening their trails to mountain bikes each year. The Wayne National Forest has also stepped up and opened 82 miles of trail in the Marietta Unit. And you won't get run over by an ORV riding there!

So, the good outweighs the not-so-good, and now it's time to ride. Tune that fork, oil that chain, mount up and read. The first, the one, and the only **Mountain Biking Ohio** is back and better than ever!

How This Book Is Organized

This book provides you with information on 36 of your future rides - fully detailed with descriptions and maps. If you have taken the time to read this introduction you may have already noticed the **Map Of Ohio's Trails** on the proceeding pages. The rides are numbered across Ohio starting in the northwest. To find a ride use the **List Of Ohio's Trails** on the facing page to match the **Trail Number** with its **Trail Name** and **Page Number** in this guide. Turn to the **Page Number** given and scope out your next adventure.

Trail Ratings

The **Trail Ratings** used in this guide are **Easy**, **Moderate**, and **Challenging**. Remember, these ratings are subjective! Almost *any* trail can be ridden by *any* rider at *any* skill level - it is just a matter of how often you will have to dismount (by choice or by force) and walk. Also, easy or less challenging trails should not be passed up by skilled riders, as they will miss some of the fastest, most fun and scenic riding in the state. However, remember to ride smart. This guide can only rate the trail; you have to rate your own abilities.

Challenging: Impress your riding buddies! Singletrack, some doubletrack. Will often include off-your-seat steep grades with extended descents and climbs, large drop-offs or jumps, off-camber, tight and twisty trails with logs, bridges and creek-crossings.

Moderate: Impress yourself! Singletrack and doubletrack. Will often include extended descents and climbs of a lesser grade, some technical riding including drop-offs, jumps, logs, or creek-crossings.

Easy: Impress your mom! Doubletrack, some singletrack. Will often include rolling hills of lesser grades, few if any extended descents and climbs, with lots of room to manoeuver and get some serious speed or relax and enjoy the scenery.

Interpreting The Ride Information

Each ride description has just the information you need to know. No trivia, no historical facts, no plant identification guide. Just the facts about what type of riding to expect and how to get there. Period.

Trail Name - Trail name, park, or forest where the trail is located.

Trail Milage - Total length of trail available in the trail system.

Trail Rating - A subjective rating to scare you off.

Overview - A brief introduction describing the area to be ridden.

Trail Description - A more detailed account of what type of trail conditions and obstacles await you.

How To Get There - A detailed description which, when combined with the location maps, will get you right to the trailhead, confusion free.

Notes - Little bits of important information like phone numbers and dates closed.

Warnings - These are boxed-in alerts which you should read to make your ride safe and enjoyable.

The Maps

Every trail described has an accompanying **Location Map**. The Location Map has two parts: 1) a square general location map to orient yourself, and 2) a circular detailed map which guides you right to the trailhead. Great care has been taken to make getting to these trails worry-free. When you combine these two maps with the **How To Get There** section a 🆃🅷 marks the spot. Read ahead and you'll spend less time in your car and more on your bike.

All trails located in state parks, state forests, and federal forests have an accompanying **Trail Map**. Trail maps show major features including trailheads, trails, roads, streams, and bodies of water. Special markings are included for trail systems which employ them, such as Scioto Trail's new numbering system.

These maps are as accurate as possible at the time of printing. However, trails change. Pay careful attention to your surroundings when you ride and you (hopefully) will not get lost. Take special care when riding trails in state and federal forests which go on for many miles. Be conservative with your mileage if it is your first time riding a trail. To err is human, but to get utterly and hopelessly lost just plain sucks. Are you directionally dyslexic? Consider buying a global positioning system (GPS). This $150 investment could save your ride.

There are no trail maps provided for most rides located on private property. Why, you ask? Unlike public land, these private trails are subject to change at the owner's whim. Many need a dynamic trail system to keep races competitive. Fortunately, these are often some of the best marked trails in the state and you will ride whatever course has last been set to race. Just follow the markers and yellow tape and you'll be fine.

Practice hills at Perry State Forest APV Area.

One final note about trails located on private property. The landowner has *complete* control over who may access the trails and when. They can deny access to *anyone* at *anytime*. Usually rules are posted and if you are not willing to follow the rules and pay the access fees then you should probably ride somewhere else. If you don't the Mountain Biking Gods will find you and hurt you. Or worse, hurt your bike. At all times, respect the property. Don't be a jerk and ruin it for everyone else. Peace.

Before You Go

I'm not your mother but I have found these things to be useful on rides:

1. This book. It's an invaluable guide.

2. Your well-tuned bike.

3. Your helmet (aka brain bucket, skid lid, your protection) for your well-tuned head. Don't like to wear a lid? Ever had a concussion? Makes a hangover feel like a good thing.

4. Water, and lots of it. Dehydration slows your response time and can make you sick as a dog. Drink before, during, and after your ride, even in the winter. Sports drinks help replace electrolytes, but they are not necessary or as cheap as good old H_2O.

5. Spare tube, pump or CO_2 cartridge, patch kit and tire levers. Nothing sucks more than humpin' a bike out from an almost epic ride.

6. A bike tool with the right size hexes for all your important parts - seat post, brakes, etc. With all that shaking things loosen up. Crashing does unexpected things to your bike too.

7. Identification. So they'll know where to ship the body.

The Companion Website

Mountain Biking Ohio was not only the first book to focus solely on mountain biking in the Buckeye State, it was also one of the first books to feature a companion website. In its brief time online www.single-track.com has had over a million visits. And like this book it too has been revised and updated. No good guide is ever complete as trails change; old ones close, new ones open, and others need volunteers for maintenance. The Mountain Biking Ohio Website allows you to be informed of these changes and makes this book a work in progress. Visit the website and you will be able to:

•Read and post new trail listings as they open

•Get current trail information and conditions

•View Ohio's race schedule

•Check trail maintenance dates

•Plan your trip

•Post pictures of your rides

•Communicate with other riders on the Message Board

•Buy, sell, or trade equipment on the free classifieds

•Get tech tips and advice

•Visit related sites

•And many other things which will keep the site fresh and relevant and keep you motivated and informed.

How To Find The Website

Just tune in to **www.single-track.com**. We're always open 24-7-365.

Mountain Bike Advocacy

Do you know who maintains the mountain biking trails that you ride on? Do you even know who owns the land? Odds are you own the land as most of Ohio's 450 miles of trail open to mountain biking are located on public property: state parks, state forests, and federal forests. And who does the maintenance? Most likely a dedicated group of government employees who are understaffed, underfunded, and overworked.

So what am I getting at? The trails need your help! Unless you get involved, progress will come very slowly, if at all. Tired of seeing so many people on your favorite trail? Tired of always coming home from a ride a muddy mess? (Remember your last fast dry ride? Probably not.) Then get involved!

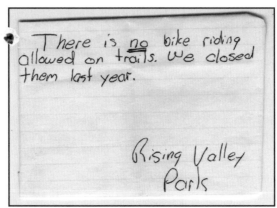

A real note left on the windshield. One less place to ride.

Listed in the back of this book are some of the organizations that are keeping your trails open and in good condition. It only takes a couple of hours a month to ensure that your trail is not closed due to "_____." Just fill in the blank: overuse, spur trails, user conflict, etc.

And guess what? Your effort will be reciprocated as the park and forest managers put their money towards an active, involved constituency. You will also get to meet some of your fellow riders. They are just like you, only you can drop them on all the climbs. Lastly, you will quickly discover that nothing feels better than flying down a piece of trail you helped build!

Want More Places To Ride?

Here are ten things you can do to get more trail opened in Ohio.

1. Join a local cycling club working to improve trail access. These groups are your allies just waiting for fresh bodies to tackle old problems and explore new possibilities. See the list of clubs in the back of this book.

2. Join the International Mountain Bicycling Association (IMBA 303-545-9026). IMBA is the one unified voice for mountain bikers across the US and world advocating responsible trail development. They also have cool schwag and benefits.

3. Volunteer your time for trail maintenance. Free help greatly impresses land managers who have limited time and resources.

4. Make your voice heard. After riding in a state park, state forest, or national forest stop by the ranger station and fill out a "Comment Card." Let them know how much you appreciate having mountain bike trail access. If there is no access at a park you visit, express your desire for future access - and your willingness to help.

5. Talk to the rangers. Impress upon them the legitimacy of the sport and show them you are a thoughtful and concerned trail user. Hey, some of these guys bike, too!

6. Talk to other trail users. Let them know you enjoy the trail just as much as they do and for the same reasons.

7. Race. Private land owners will continue to open trails if they think there is money to be made. So far this has produced some of the best trails in Ohio.

8. Support your local bike shop and find out what they are doing to improve trail access. The math is simple: more trails = more sales.

9. Follow the rules of the trail - ride open trail only, leave no trace, control your bicycle, always yield trail, never spook animals, and plan

ahead to keep existing trails open and in good shape.

10. Encourage other mountain bikers to get involved. Enthusiasm is addictive!

The Best of The Best

Okay, now you have 36 trails to choose from and only time for one ride. Where do you go? Well, that depends on what type of riding you're in the mood for. So here goes a rather random rambling of the best of Ohio.

•**Best State Park Ride** - Caesar Creek State Park (Climbs, creeks, dropoffs, forests, open fields, and all killer singletrack. See page 32.)

•**Best Place to Lose Your Mountain Biking Virginity** - Hueston Woods State Park (Gentle yet hard, you'll remember the ride like it was prom night. See page 28.)

•**Best National Forest Ride** - Monday Creek, Wayne National Forest, Athens Unit (With 72 miles of trail you can't go wrong. Although the Marietta Unit, with no ORVs and 82 miles of trail, stands poised to dethrone Monday Creek. See page 60.)

•**Best State Forest Ride** - Pike State Forest (Dares you to go just a little faster until, wham! You're still flying along; your bike, however, stopped at that last tree. See page 40.)

•**Best Technical Ride** - Vulture's Knob (You will ride, you will fall, and you will love it. Thank you, may I have another? See page 81.)

•**Best Fall Colors** - Lake Hope State Park (New England has nothing on this place. See page 58.)

•**Best Place To Race** - Mickey's Mountain (Crosscountry, dual slalom, downhill, hill climb and trials. They cover it all. See page 74.)

•**Best Family Ride** - Findley State Park (Nothing too scary and a place to swim! See page 86.)

•**Best Hardcore Kickbutt Full Day of Riding** - Scioto Trail State Park and Forest (Hills, rocks, creeks, singletrack, vistas, fire roads, and more hills. It just gets better every time you ride it. See page 48.)

How trails really get built. By volunteers.

Map Symbols

I-71	- Interstate 71
US 23	- U.S. Route 23
SR 278	- State Route 278
FR 105	- Forest Road 105
CR 193	- County Road 193
TR 211	- Township Road 211

 Mountain Bike Trail
Unpaved Road
Paved Road
Stream

⬤ Water

10 General Location

TH Trailhead

N

0   Miles   1.0

Milage Scale

Kelley's Island State Park

5 miles / Easy

Overview: Kelley's Island is a family place and the trails reflect it. If you are going just to mountain bike it is hardly worth the price of admission (the ferry ride costs about $12 for you and your bike). However, if you are already going to the island to enjoy a summer weekend with the family bring the bikes. The trails are multiple use so expect bumpy terrain and a leisurely, scenic ride.

Trail Description: The North Shore Loop Trail skirts a large quarry and the shore of Lake Erie. It has some very nice spots to stop and have lunch while looking out across that vast body of water. The 1.5 mile trail is mostly flat with just a few rocks and roots to keep you on your toes. The trailhead is located next to the state park camping area.

Less then a mile away from the North Shore Loop the East Quarry Trail is situated in the middle of the island. It too is flat and forms a horseshoe around the east end of a large quarry. The water collected in it is a tempting ice blue on those hot summer days but swimming is prohibited. The trail does descend into the quarry but dead-ends at its west end. Other trails crisscross on the southern side of the quarry and are laid out like city streets totaling about 3.5 miles. Again, nothing too exciting but if you're already in the area, go for it.

How To Get There: This is the only ride you need a boat to get to. From Cleveland take I-90/I-80 or SR 2 west to Sandusky or Lakeside which is closer. Catch a ferry to Kelleys Island. Ferrys run on the half hour at peak season. Expect to pay about $12 for you and your bike, $16 for your car. North Shore Loop Trailhead is found at the end of Division St. Main East Quarry Trailhead is on Wood St. Unless you're camping there is no need to take your car across on the ferry as the island is tiny.

Notes: Park @ 419-746-2546. Emergency @ 911.

Why? Because lifting weights is boring.

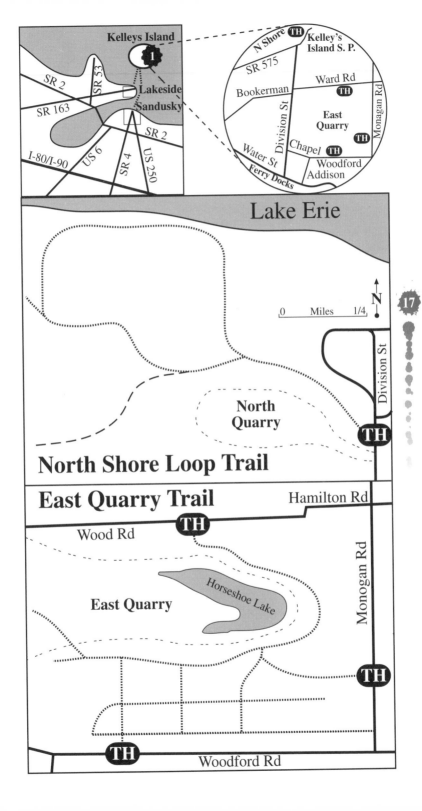

Kelleys Island

1

SR 2
SR 53
SR 163
I-80/I-90
US 6
SR 4
US 250
SR 2

Lakeside
Sandusky

N Shore **TH**
Kelley's Island S. P.
SR 575
Bookerman
Ward Rd **TH**
Monagan Rd
Division St
East Quarry **TH**
Chapel **TH**
Water St
Ferry Docks
Woodford
Addison

Lake Erie

N
0 Miles 1/4

17

Division St

North Quarry

TH

North Shore Loop Trail

East Quarry Trail

Hamilton Rd

TH

Wood Rd

Monogan Rd

Horseshoe Lake

East Quarry

TH

TH

Woodford Rd

Maumee State Forest
APV Trail

5 miles / Easy

Overview: Currently *the* ride of northwest Ohio. Glaciers really did a number on mountain bikers in this part of the state, but the Ohio Division of Forestry has provided one solid ride. The Maumee APV Area has a sandy-loam soil with virtually no change in elevation, but is a fun ride none-the-less. You get out of this ride exactly what you put into it, so go have fun on those whoop-dee-dos!

Trail Description: The Maumee offers 5 miles of shared APV, snow mobile, and mountain biking trails. On the east side of parking area APVs have carved out a series of jumps and banked turns. These are worth the extra effort it takes to crank and hit them with speed. One to three foot undulating hills spaced one after another makes you feel like you are rolling on ocean waves. It also makes for a good workout of those weak forearms!

The west side loop trail winds through a mature pine plantation and is generally well marked. The area is so small it is virtually impossible to get lost, even with spur trails. It does get muddy so spring riding is probably out. The trails are posted as one way travel but you'll quickly see many APV's ignore this.

How To Get There: You would think that with roads laid out like a big grid it would be easy to find this place. Not so, as all the roads look the same your first time there. And original names like Road A, B, C and 1, 2, 3 don't help. From Toledo take I-90/I-80 west to SR 2 west. From SR 2 turn left on CR 2 heading south. The parking area is just past Road D on the left. From Bowling Green the easiest route is to follow SR 64 north to Archbold Whitehouse Road in Whitehouse. Go west on Archbold Whitehouse then north on CR 2.

Notes: Forest @ 419-822-3052. Emergency @ 911.

APV Warning! These trails get intense use from APV riders who are generally friendly to mountain bikers. When an APV approaches, remember to move completely off the trail, if possible, maintaining a good line of sight. It has become customary using hand signals to sign the number in your group to the APV riders so everyone will know what to expect. Summer riding is best as is takes the area a while to dry out in the spring and the APVs churn up a lot of mud. Weekends are busiest. The trails are closed from December 1 to March 31 to reduce erosion. One final word of caution: this state forest is open to most forms of hunting. If you ride during the late fall wear bright colors and feel free to make lots of noise. Earth tones and silence may kill you.

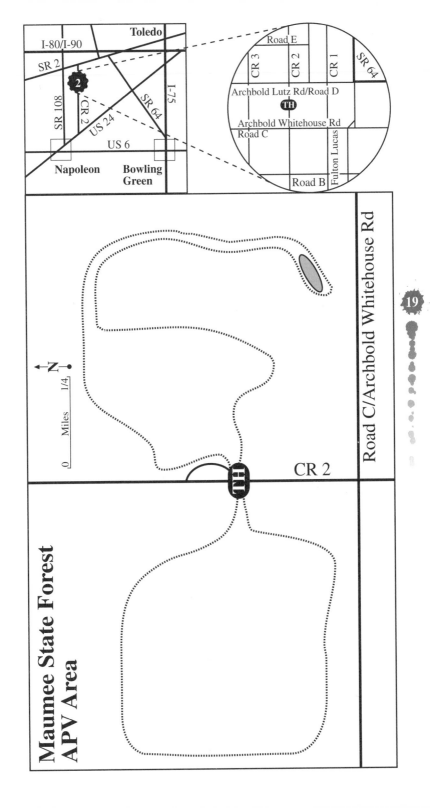

Maumee State Forest
APV Area

Toledo
I-80/I-90
SR 2
SR 108
CR 2
US 24
SR 64
I-75
US 6
Napoleon
Bowling Green

2

Road E
CR 3
CR 2
CR 1
SR 64
Archbold Lutz Rd/Road D
TH
Archbold Whitehouse Rd
Road C
Fulton Lucas
Road B

Road C/Archbold Whitehouse Rd

CR 2

TH

N

Miles
0   1/4

19

Oakwood Park

3.5 miles / Easy

Overview: More proof that small town life is better. The residents of Napoleon have what millions in Ohio's largest cities can only dream about: their own mountain bike trail! And while it only spans a few miles and has an elevation change no more than 50 feet it's still a great local resource.

Trail Description: This fun trail has about 3.5 miles of singletrack built with bikes in mind. The first thing you will notice are the rock-solid bridges spanning the small ravines throughout the trail. Making good use of small space, the trail follows two creek valleys within Oakwood Park. The bridges open up hillsides which would otherwise be too tricky to build trail on. The trail follows Van Hyning Creek upstream in a clockwise loop before dropping down a set of switchbacks to doubleback beside the creek. A second loop can be added by either riding across the creek or following a narrow bridge.

The riding is fast and twisting among old hardwoods and sycamore trees and the abandoned classic cars are a bizarre twist too, so keep your eyes open. The creek bottom probably floods so it's best to avoid the area after rainfall. This trail is marked as being directional but spur trails often intersect, so it's easy to find yourself going in the wrong direction. As the city expands the trail system, this may become even more confusing. One other thing you'll probably notice on this trail is the friendliness of the other riders. Say hello and they just might offer to buy you lunch. It's gotta be the small town life.

How To Get There: From Toledo take US 24 west to Napoleon. After US 6 joins US 24 begin looking for Industrial. Exit Industrial south and take the first right on Independence. Take a left on Oakwood and look for the Oakwood Park sign.

Notes: Great local resource but not enough trail for a road trip. Park @ 419-592-1555. Emergency @ 911.

One of the many bridges at Oakwood Park.

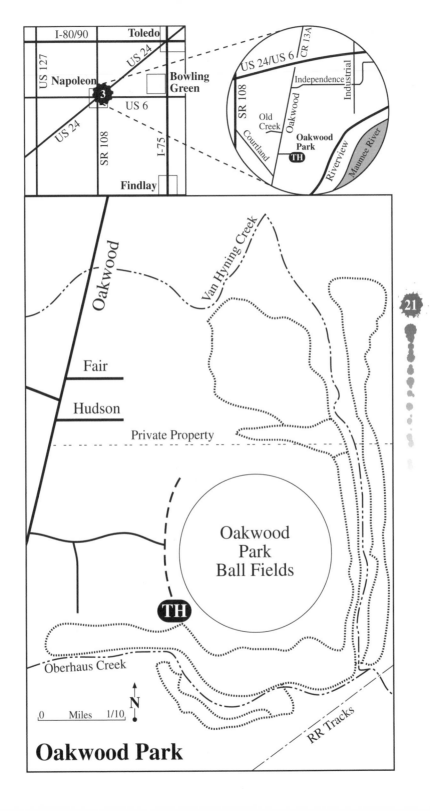

Oakwood Park

I-80/90 Toledo
US 127 US 24
Napoleon **3** Bowling Green
US 6
US 24 SR 108 I-75
Findlay

US 24/US 6 CR 13A
SR 108 Independence Industrial
Oakwood
Old Creek
Courtland Oakwood Park **TH** Riverview Maumee River

Oakwood
Van Hyning Creek
21
Fair
Hudson
Private Property
Oakwood Park Ball Fields
TH
Oberhaus Creek
N
0 Miles 1/10
RR Tracks

Mary Jane Thurston State Park

6 miles / Easy

Overview: With so few places to ride in northwest Ohio the North Turkeyfoot Area of Mary Jane Thurston State Park is one more place to get that bike on real dirt. However, most of the 6 miles of trail available are a grassy, bumpy, brutal ride without much to see. If you're really desperate the northern section of the park does have a couple of miles of decent trail.

Trail Description: The area open to bikes is split by North Turkeyfoot Creek. Pheasant Loop on the north is your best bet for a fun ride. Descending down to, then following beside the creek, the trail is wide and flat. Being so close to the creek the trail probably floods and has the potential for mud. In the shade of the big hardwoods you might spot some nice wildflowers. The trails south of the creek are very bumpy and really suitable only for horses and hunting. They are wide and well marked should you have lots of energy to burn. Those bordering the Maumee River are your best bet. Don't bother with Racoon or Opossum Loop. If you do visit make sure to go look at the old steel bridge crossing the creek while you're there. It's the coolest thing about the place.

How To Get There: From Toledo take I-475 to US 24 west. You will be on US 24 for about 25 miles. *Do not* turn on SR 578 south to go to the state park! Stay on US 24 to the North Turkeyfoot Area. Parking and a kiosk is just beyond the small town of Texas.

Notes: Park @ 419-832-7662. Emergency @ 911. Closed for hunting November 1 - March 1.

Dogwood Trail at Beaver Creek State Park.

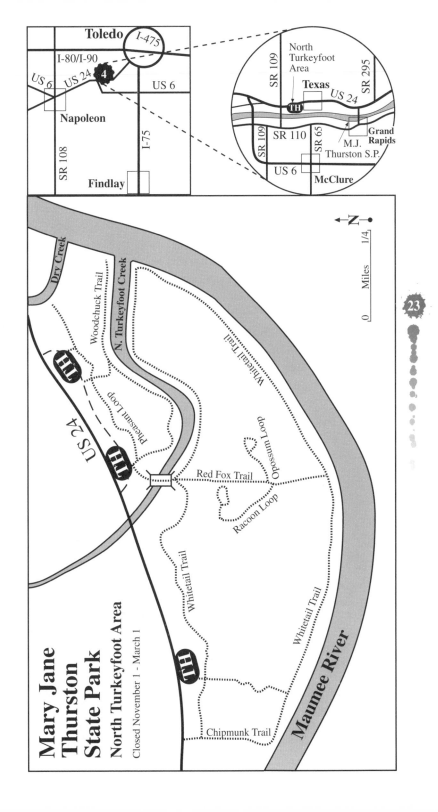

Mary Jane Thurston State Park
North Turkeyfoot Area

Closed November 1 - March 1

N

0   1/4
Miles

Toledo   I-475

I-80/I-90   4

US 6   US 24   US 6

Napoleon

SR 108   I-75

Findlay

North Turkeyfoot Area

SR 109   **Texas**   SR 295
US 24

TH

SR 109   SR 110   SR 65   **Grand Rapids**
M.J. Thurston S.P.

US 6   **McClure**

Dry Creek

Woodchuck Trail

N. Turkeyfoot Creek

Whitetail Trail

Pheasant Loop

US 24

TH

TH

Opossum Loop

Red Fox Trail

Racoon Loop

Whitetail Trail

Whitetail Trail

TH

Chipmunk Trail

Maumee River

23

Handlebar Hollow

2 miles / Easy

Overview: Once again, a smaller city in Ohio is ahead of the pack when it comes to recreation planning. Case-in-point Findlay's Handlebar Hollow. This place even has a cool name! They've even named sections of trail to let you know what you're in for. The Snake. Thunder Hollow. Devils Hole. Are we still in Ohio? The answer is yes but there's no need for you adrenaline junkies to load up the Yakima just yet. This is a beginner loop from start to finish. Elevation change is maybe 20 feet and total length is about 2 miles. But if you live in the area and want to try out that new toy you got, this is the place.

Trail Description: Handlebar Hollow winds its way along the north side of the Blanchard River through a city greenway. This directional trail makes good use of a small space carving in and out of some ancient sycamore trees just beside the river. Its proximity to the river means it is closed when conditions are wet, so plan ahead. The trail is very well marked and has a great kiosk at the entrance so there's absolutely no chance of getting lost. You will find opportunities to build your skills with some creative twists, turns, dips, and straight-aways build for speed. The only down side is when the wind is from the southwest you become extremely aware that the Findlay wastewater treatment plant is on the opposite side of the river. It can make gulping down those lungfulls of air kinda hard.

How To Get There: From the north or south follow I-75 into Findlay and take the US 224/Trenton Avenue exit. On West Trenton take the first right on Broad then a left on Howard. Turn right on Fox and you will see the trailhead sign.

Notes: Good local resource but not enough trail for a road trip. Maintenance by Hancock Handlebars Bicycle Club. Hancock Park District @ 419-424-7275. Findlay Recreation Department @ 419-424-7176. Emergency @ 911.

Voted the best trailhead sign in all of Ohio.

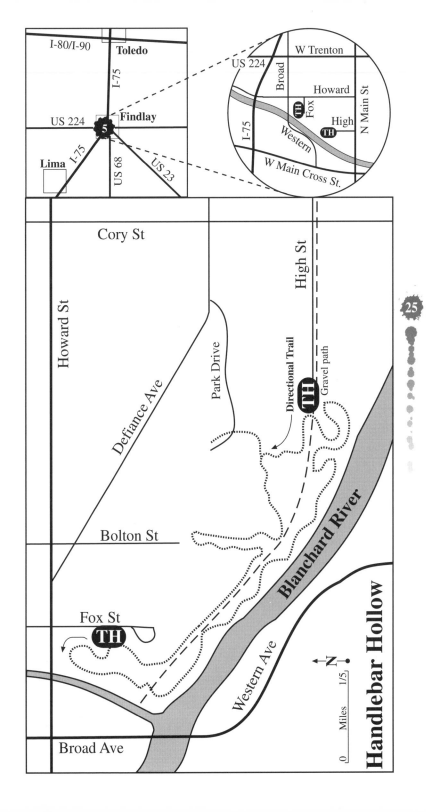

I-80/I-90 **Toledo**
I-75
US 224 **Findlay**
5
Lima I-75 US 68 US 23

US 224 W Trenton
Broad
Howard
I-75 **TH** Fox
Western **TH** High N Main St
W Main Cross St.

Cory St

Howard St

High St

Defiance Ave

Park Drive

Directional Trail

TH Gravel path

Bolton St

Blanchard River

Fox St

TH

Western Ave

N

Miles 1/5
0

Broad Ave

Handlebar Hollow

25

Alum Creek State Park

7 miles / Easy - Moderate

Overview: Mud, roots, and ruts. Alum Creek is the closest thing to classic East Coast riding you are likely to find in Ohio. The twisting singletrack can be slick and muddy, and somewhere there is a root with your name on it. When dry, fast and gnarly downhills, more than its share of creek-crossings, and a lakeside view, make this *the* ride of central Ohio. The north trails are almost entirely wooded and treefall is common; expect to dig your big chainring into a log or two. Wet conditions and overuse have hurt these trails so you might avoid the area until midsummer.

Trail Description: The serious trails are all north of the parking lot with the best following the shores of the lake and its numerous tributaries. They are composed of twisting singletrack and generally stay in better shape as water flows across them and does not pool. If you follow the main outer loop (from the parking lot go counter-clockwise and keep taking rights) you will hit most of the good trails available. This loop is about 5 miles long. The northwestern most sections can be slop although volunteers are working to provide some relief. Expect more new singletrack like the short section to the left of the main parking area.

A 2 mile beginner loop of flat open riding is located across from the parking area and is a good place to warm up or cool down. Often muddy.

How To Get There: Alum Creek State Park is located north of Columbus, west of I-71. From I-71 exit east onto Polaris Parkway. Follow Polaris Parkway north and it will become Worthington Galena Road. Follow Worthington Galena Road north to Lewis Center and take a left. Follow it to the trailhead, about 1 mile down on the right. You can also reach Lewis Center Road from US 23 on the West.

Notes: Don't even try riding here until mid-summer unless you like mud. Park @ 614-548-4631. Emergency @ 911. Maintenance by COMBO.

Amateur racing is where it's at. Here it's at Hueston Woods State Park.

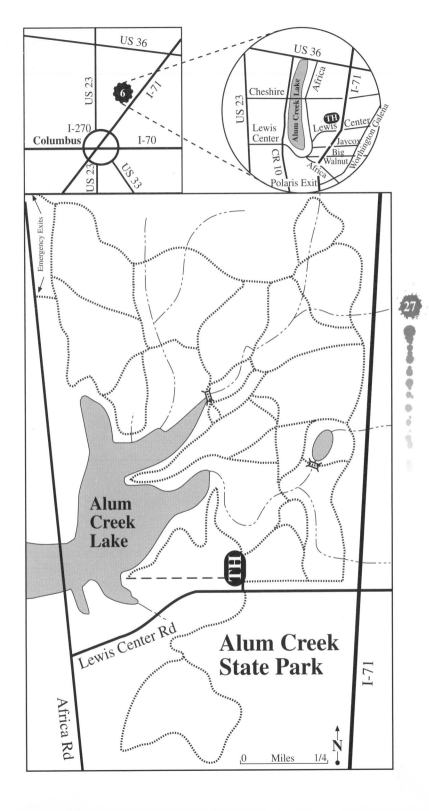

US 36

US 23

I-270
Columbus
I-70

US 23

US 33

I-71

6

US 36

Cheshire

Africa

I-71

US 23

Alum Creek Lake

TH
Lewis Center

Lewis

Center

CR 10

Jaycox

Big
Walnut

Africa

Polaris Exit

Worthington Galena

Emergency Exits

27

**Alum
Creek
Lake**

TH

Lewis Center Rd

**Alum Creek
State Park**

I-71

Africa Rd

0   Miles   1/4

N

Hueston Woods State Park

10 miles / Easy - Moderate

Overview: Bordering the northwest side of Acton Lake this park has a diverse variety of trails built strictly for mountain biking. There is a little bit of everything from flat and rolling to tight and technical, all singletrack. Other than the possibility of getting lost because there are almost too many trails to choose from, there aren't many down-sides to the place. The majority of trail is beginner to intermediate in difficulty. This is a good place to build your skills, and one of the only spots in Ohio to rent a mountain bike at the trailhead.

Trail Description: Across from the parking area there are approximately 8 miles of interconnected singletrack trails surrounded by a 2 mile loop. The main trailhead is at the intersection of Loop Road and Hedge Row Road. A set of power lines bisects the trails north and south. North of the power lines a variety of moderately challenging trails work their way up, down and across a number of hills. A fast hard-packed trail follows the power lines and provides the necessary wide-open extended hills to get tons of speed! South of the power lines are a variety of good trails for beginning riders, complete with skill-building short drops, covered with plenty of soft dirt to land in. Plush.

Just north of the parking area lies a new section of trails which wind through a narrow wooded hillside, bordered by a day use area on the west, a service road on the north, and Loop Road on the east. This adds a little over 2 miles of fun intermediate level riding.

How To Get There: From central and northeast Ohio take I-70 west past Dayton to US 127 south. Follow US 127 south to SR 732 in Eaton. Follow SR 732 south. Once you cross SR 725 begin looking for the sign for Camden-College Corner Road. Turn right onto Camden-College Corner Road and follow it for 1.5 miles until you come to Hedge Row Road on your left. Follow this until you intersect with Loop Road. The parking lot is on the left and the trailhead is on the right. From Cincinnati take US 27 north to Oxford and SR 732. Follow SR 732 north 5 miles to the main park entrance. Once in the park, follow Loop Road to Group Camping and the intersection of Row Road. Just look for the mountain bike rental stand.

Notes: Bike rental and power grub available from the mountain bike rental stand. Park @ 513-523-6347. Emergency @ 911.

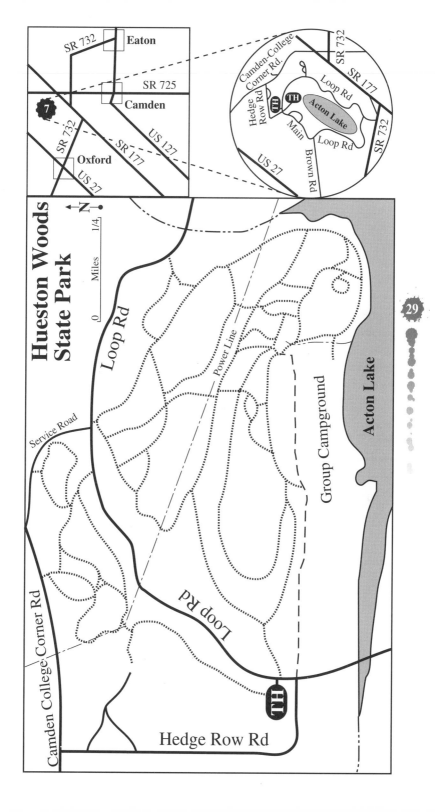

Hueston Woods State Park

N

0   1/4
Miles

Loop Rd

SR 732   Eaton

SR 725

Camden

7

SR 732   US 127

SR 177

Oxford

US 27

Camden-College Corner Rd.

SR 732

SR 177

Loop Rd

Hedge Row Rd

TH   TH

Acton Lake

Main

Loop Rd

SR 732

US 27

Brown Rd

Camden College Corner Rd

Service Road

Power Line

Loop Rd

Group Campground

Acton Lake

Hedge Row Rd

TH

29

Harbin Park

5 miles / Easy - Moderate

Overview: Another city in Ohio has embraced mountain biking as a legitimate use of park property. Cleveland take note! Fairfield's Harbin Park has even hosted a series of summer races for the past few years. The 5 miles of trail range from open grassy hills to technical wooded singletrack, and are deceptively challenging.

Trail Description: The trail partially follows a fitness course which is open and grassy and includes a number of big hills. On a clear day the view is a must see. While this course may seem a little tame at first you will come to respect these hills and love the speed they grant. After circling the area you will find the majority of technical singletrack is in the north part of the park. Trails cut in and out of brushy hillsides in a confusing criss-cross. If you're not familiar with the trails follow the race course arrows. When dry these trails are fast with tight turns, short drops, off camber climbs, and fallen logs everywhere. Switchbacks make the most out of the small valleys, wrapping the trails down one side and up and around the other. There are even a few steep extended climbs to give your lungs a workout.

How To Get There: From Cincinnati follow I-275 to US 127 north. After you cross John Gray Road begin looking for Hunter Drive. Turn left on Hunter which ends in Harbin Park. From the north or east it's easiest to hit the I-275 loop west around Cincinnati and exit US 127 north. You can enter the trail at a number of places. The park is too small to get lost in so enjoy!

Notes: Good local resource but wouldn't make a long road trip to ride here. Park @ 513-867-5348. Emergency @ 911.

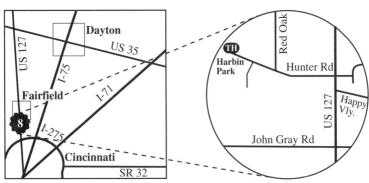

Landen-Deerfield Park

3.5 miles / Easy

Overview: Wow! This park gets the award for best use of a small space. Packed into just a few acres of wooded property is 3.5 miles of tight and twisty singletrack. This wild trail sometimes feels like a ride at Cedar Point. It cuts back on itself again and again and in a group ride keeping up with your friends makes whiplash is a definite threat.

Trail Description: Don't expect much change in elevation as this ride only has a few hills to conquer. However, you will get to explore every inch of the hills it does have. This dizzying trail can really get the heartrate monitor beeping if you take laps at speed. Considering the trail is bordered on all sides by suburbia, it's in good shape. And while it runs beside, above and even through a small stream, potential trail damage has been avoided by closing the trail when it's wet or icy. Probably not a good winter or spring ride. Another smart feature of this trail is that it is very well marked, with color blazes, arrows, and even maps located throughout the trail system. If you get lost here you probably shouldn't leave your home unaccompanied.

How To Get There: From Cincinnati take I-71 north to the Fields Ertel exit. Take a right (east) on Fields Ertel Road then a left (north) on US 22/ SR 3. This is also signed as Montgomery Road. After about 3 miles the park will be on your left. The trailhead is in the back and marked.

Notes: Good local resource but not enough trail for a road trip. Park @ 513-695-1109. Emergency @ 911.

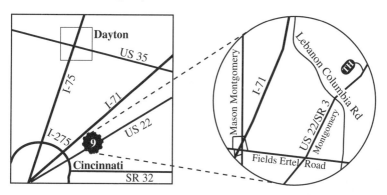

Caesar Creek State Park

13 miles / Easy - Moderate

Overview: Hugging the east side of Caesar Creek Lake are 10 miles of moderately technical singletrack. Split by Ward Road, the northern loop never gets boring, with numerous small creek-crossings, steep climbs and descents, and technical sections with definite endo-potential. The southern section can be more typical Ohio mud-and-slop, interspersed with funky technical off-the-back descents, hike-a-bike steep climbs, and one potentially exciting creek-crossing. A new loop is also available south of the main trails which is perfect for newbies. Set in a beautiful hardwood forest with a lakeside view, Caesar Creek is probably the best state park ride.

Trail Description: Ward Road makes a good departure point for both the north and south trails. Aside from a 2 mile flat loop, part of which is road riding, the north trail is solid singletrack. Lots of creek-crossings, winding ascents and descents, a few technical drop-offs, and one straight drop of about 60 feet with almost no run-out -- check out the dings in the trees at the bottom when the stock brakes just couldn't cut it. New singletrack bypasses some of the old open field riding with smart, scary descents to a lakeside view.

Like any trail in Ohio, the south trail can be slop but has some surprisingly challenging technical ascents and descents, and a great 20 foot wide creek crossing. South of the creek, several loops have been cut off of the main trail which is starting to get Alum Creek Syndrome: too many trails in too small of a space. North of the creek a challenging new lakeside trail now connects you to the Ward Road trailhead. This section totals about 6 miles.

50 Springs is 70% doubletrack and a good place for a ride with the entire family. A crosscountry ski trail in the winter, this 3 mile loop works its way out and back a small peninsula. There are a number of nice lakeside views and places to stop and enjoy them. The east side of the loop is more singletrack in nature, and has some fast twists and turns carving through the cedars but nothing very serious.

How To Get There: From I-71 take SR 73 west 2+ miles to Brimstone Road for the middle or north trailhead or a little farther to Harveysburg Road for the south trailhead. For the middle trailhead turn right on Brimstone then left on Ward Road. The trailhead is at the end of Ward Road. For the north trailhead follow Brimstone Road, cross Ward Road, and continue on Mills Road. This will end at Center Road. Turn left and follow Center Road to the parking lot on the right. For 50 Springs keep going west on SR 73 and look for the signs on the left. Park in the first lot on your left.

Notes: Park @ 513-897-3055. Emergency @ 911. Volunteer maintenance by West Chester Cyclery, International Pro Cyclery, others.

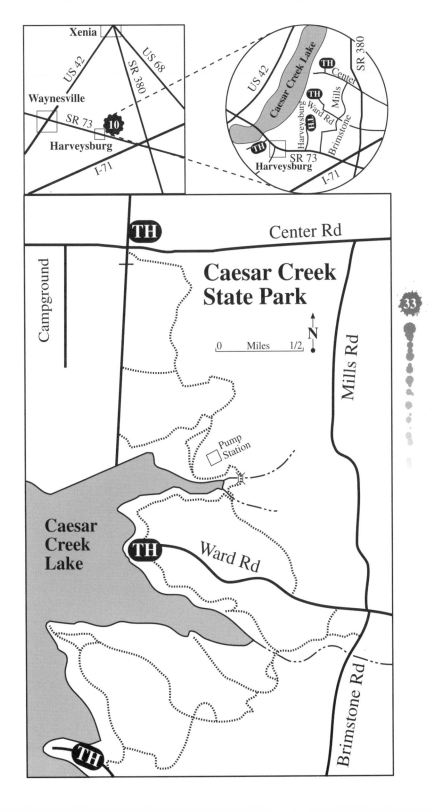

Xenia

US 42
US 68
SR 380

Waynesville

SR 73
10

Harveysburg

I-71

Caesar Creek Lake
US 42
SR 380
TH Center
TH Mills
Harveysburg Ward Rd
TH
TH
SR 73
Harveysburg
I-71

TH

Center Rd

Campground

Caesar Creek
State Park

0   Miles   1/2

N

Mills Rd

Pump
Station

TH

Caesar
Creek
Lake

Ward Rd

Brimstone Rd

TH

Deer Creek State Park

1.2 miles / Easy

Overview: Along with 18 holes of golf you can now enjoy a short bike ride at Deer Creek State Park and Resort. The 1.2 mile trail is rolling to flat with lakeside views, followed by open field riding. A good beginners loop and a nice start for the park.

Trail Description: This new trail was built for bikes and provides a gentle introduction to the sport. The doubletrack trail even has a few hills which the novice rider might find a little intimidating. Remember, keep your butt back and don't jam on those brakes. Riding counter-clockwise the trail enters the woods staying just above the lake. Out of the woods the trail heads through open fields bordered by thorn bushes waiting to make you bleed. You better hope they keep it trimmed back. The flat upland trail has the potetial to hold water so spring riding might be out.

34

How To Get There: From Columbus take I-71 south to US 62 south. Follow US 62 through Mt. Sterling to SR 207. SR 207 runs south of Deer Creek Lake. After you cross over a tributary of the lake begin looking for Crownover Mill Road on the left. Take Crownover Mill and follow the signs to the beach entrance. Take the first left. The trailhead is marked and at the end of the road.

Notes: Park @ 740-869-3124. Emergency @ 911.

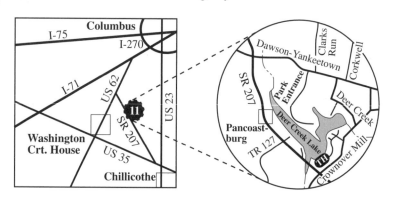

Two racers in a battle for position at Ceasar Creek State Park.

East Fork State Park

4.4 miles / Easy - Moderate

Overview: Two well maintained, connected loops wind their way through a small portion of the bottomland hardwood forest bordering East Fork Lake. The area is mostly flat with only about 100 foot change in elevation as the trail crosses small drainages. This is a very tight singletrack trail which keeps the rider either alert, or on the ground with their bar-end wrapped around a tree. When it is wet it can be very sloppy. A fun ride close to Cincinnati but skilled riders might get bored quickly.

Trail Description: There are two connecting loops, each about 2.2 miles in length, for about 4.4 miles total. The loop connected to the trailhead is a lesson in getting speed out of corners as it winds through a thick stand of small trees. Count on ramming at least one if you're trying to make time. Further on, the trail opens up some, with a few small hills and a fun switch-back. The next connected loop is located on a small peninsula into the lake. It's also tight singletrack with more hills as it negotiates a number of drainages. Both loops can be completed in less than 30 minutes. Maybe not Ohio's biggest adrenaline rush, but definitely worth a look.

How To Get There: East Fork State Park is about 25 miles east of Cincinnati off SR 125. From the north follow I-71 or I-75 south to the I-275 loop. Take the loop I-275 east and exit SR 125 east. The park entrance is at SR 222. Enter on Park Road. The trailhead is just beyond the park office on the left. Follow the short gravel road between two ponds to the parking area.

Notes: Do not ride on the bridal or hiking trails. Park @ 513-734-4323. Emergency @ 911. Maintenance by Queen City Wheels and KYMBA.

You're never too young, or old, to help out.

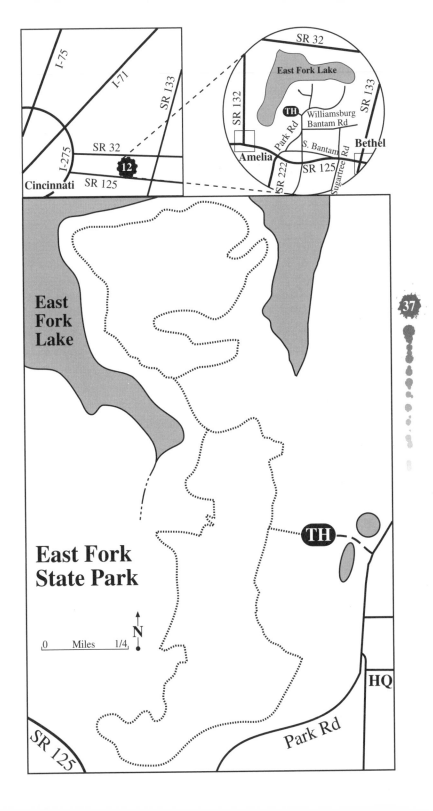

I-75

I-71

SR 133

SR 32

SR 32

East Fork Lake

SR 132

TH

Williamsburg
Bantam Rd

S. Bantam

SR 133

Bethel

SR 133

I-275

12

Park Rd

SR 222

Sugartree Rd

Cincinnati

SR 125

Amelia

SR 125

**East
Fork
Lake**

37

**East Fork
State Park**

TH

0   Miles   1/4

N

HQ

SR 125

Park Rd

Rocky Fork State Park

2 miles / Moderate

Overview: Like its neighbor Paint Creek, Rocky Fork has lots of potential for providing good mountain biking. The first trail open to mountain biking was built by a scout troop and they picked a nice spot. This short 2 mile loop has great lakeside views as it twists along a number of small tributaries that feed the lake and your need for speed.

Trail Description: The trail forms a loop with a small amount of overlap at the beginning. Sections of the trail have a feel similar to the riding at Ceasar Creek, but without the mud. You'll spend much of your time working down, across, and back out of the small valleys which border the lake. Some of these are technically challenging with steep drops and climbs. In the open and carving along the hillsides you can really get a good clip going. It looks like there will be expansion in the near future which is good as the current length of the ride isn't worth the road trip. Keep your eye on this place.

How To Get There: From Cincinnati take US 50 east to Hillsboro. In Hillsboro turn right on SR 124. Follow SR 124 east to Chestnut Road. Go left on Chestnut and left again White Lane. Look for the Fisherman's Wharf sign. Follow White Lane to the end and the marked trailhead. From Columbus take I-71 south to US 62 south to Hillsboro. From Hillsboro follow the above directions.

Notes: Park @ 937-393-4284. Emergency @ 911. Maintenance by Scout Troop 6, Cincinnati @ 1-800-872-6887.

If you ride at Denison leave your racoon at home! It's the law.

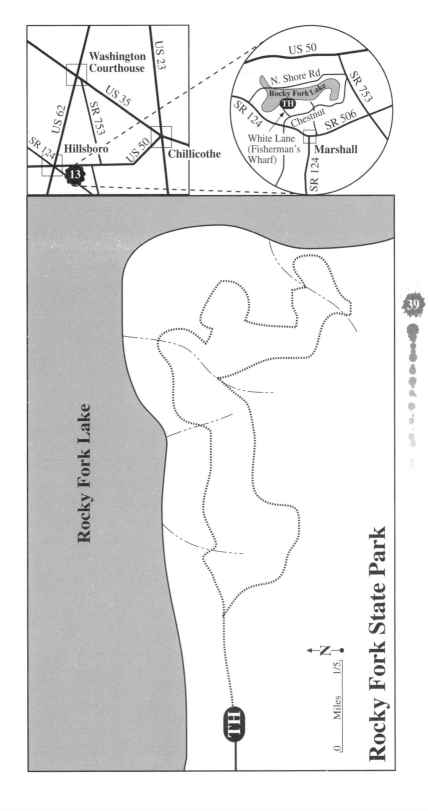

Washington Courthouse

US 23

US 35

US 62

SR 753

SR 124

Hillsboro

US 50

13

Chillicothe

US 50

N. Shore Rd

SR 753

Rocky Fork Lake

TH

SR 124

Chestnut

SR 506

White Lane (Fisherman's Wharf)

Marshall

SR 124

39

Rocky Fork Lake

N

0   Miles   1/5

TH

Rocky Fork State Park

Pike State Forest
APV Area

15 miles / Challenging

Overview: This is probably the best maintained and best marked system of APV (All-Purpose Vehicle) trails in the state. Due to the big hills (mountains) and potential for unplanned dismounts (crashes) these trails will appeal to more advanced (crazy) riders. Like other state forests, expect grueling climbs, great descents, and tons of speed (fun, fun, fun). So why does it get an advanced rating? Some of the climbs are lung-burners and some of the downhills are death on two wheels. You'll also get to experience a whopping 460 foot change in elevation peaking at 1200 feet. Are we living large in Ohio or what?

Trail Description: After even more work and rerouting the trail system is in excellent shape. The 15 miles of trail look as though they were laid out with the mountain biker in mind. They are well marked and numbered so getting lost is not a problem. Only a few trails are of the full-throttle variety, simply plowing straight up a hill. Instead, most offer a winding path, which, while grueling, are do-able. These are some of the best trails to bomb down at considerable speed. There are, however, a few places where you should just leave your brain at the top of the hill and go for it. Remember, collarbones heal. Following the outer loop clockwise is a long, tough, rewarding ride. Slick and sticky riding when it's wet but fast and dusty when dry. Also, this APV area actually *likes* having mountain bikers riding their trails so if you see someone who looks official, tell them thanks!

How To Get There: Pike State Forest APV Area is located southwest of Chillicothe. From north Ohio take US 23 south though Chillicothe to SR 32 west. Follow SR 32 five miles to SR 124 north. Follow SR 124 about 15 miles to the trailhead north of the road. Look for the Forest Service sign. From Cincinnati follow SR 32 east to SR 41 north. Go right on SR 124 and the trailhead will be about 3 miles down on the left.

Notes: Forest @ 740-493-2441. Emergency @ 911. Camping at Paint Creek where you can ride some more! Trails closed December 1 to March 31.

APV Warning! These trails get intense use from APV riders who are generally friendly to mountain bikers. When an APV approaches, remember to move completely off the trail, if possible, maintaining a good line of sight. It has become customary using hand signals to sign the number in your group to the APV riders so everyone will know what to expect. Summer riding is best as is takes the area a while to dry out in the spring and the APVs churn up a lot of mud. Weekends are busiest. The trails are closed from December 1 to March 31 to reduce erosion. One final word of caution: this state forest is open to most forms of hunting. If you ride during the late fall wear bright colors and feel free to make lots of noise. Earth tones and silence may kill you.

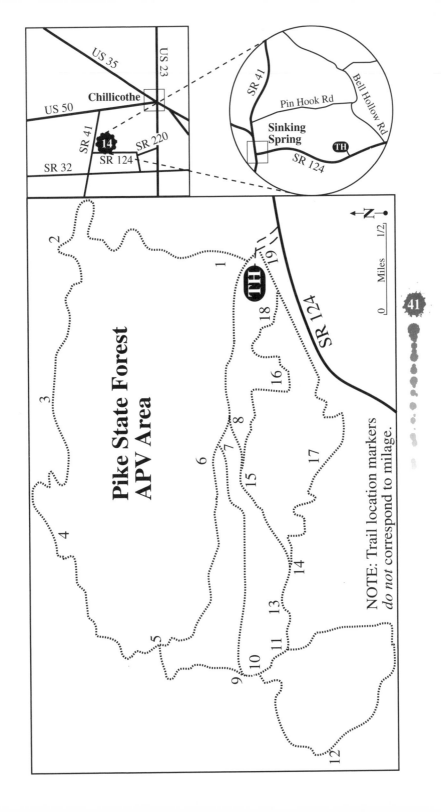

Pike State Forest APV Area

NOTE: Trail location markers *do not correspond to milage.*

US 35
US 23
Chillicothe
US 50
SR 41
14
SR 220
SR 32
SR 124

SR 41
Pin Hook Rd
Bell Hollow Rd
Sinking Spring
TH
SR 124

TH
SR 124

N

0   Miles   1/2

41

Paint Creek State Park

14 miles / Easy - Moderate

Overview: This park, relatively close to both Columbus and Cincinnati, offers a number of easy to moderately difficult loops. As one of the only parks in Ohio with a mountain biker on staff, it shows in the improved quality and diversity of the trails. Wide, open rolling singletrack make up the majority of the north and south loops but short technical trails are available to challenge the experienced rider. More challenging trails are marked as so. You've been warned.

Trail Description: About 14 miles of trail are divided into two main loops, one north of Taylor Road and one south. The 3 mile north loop is generally wide, hilly, and fast if it's dry. If it's wet, get ready to swim. This is a good trail for beginners. If you begin to feel more adventurous, two 1 mile singletrack loops spur off the main trail offering technical and rocky riding. A number of tricky creek-crossings provide the necessary element of danger.

The main south loop can be 4 to 6.5 miles, depending on where you decide to turn left and right. These trails are much improved with a definable line, solid base, and the cobblestone paths are gone, mostly. The three new singletracks have great twists and turns through hardwoods and along the lake. There is some exciting offcamber riding and great scenery. For serious riders this is a huge improvement and the new trails should last a long, long time. If you haven't been to Paint Creek in a while, these improvements make it worth a return trip. And no, the scenic view and picnic area aren't worth the detour. But who cares?

How To Get There: Paint Creek State Park is located off US 50 in southwest Ohio. To reach the trailhead take Rapid Forge Road north following it past the first park entrance to Taylor Road on the left. Follow Taylor Road down to the parking lot on the right. The north loop trailhead is there. The south trailhead is located 0.25 mile back up Taylor Road; you will see it on the left as you are driving in. Look out for bikers on the road coming to and from the trail.

Notes: Park @ 937-365-1401. Emergency @ 937-365-1401.

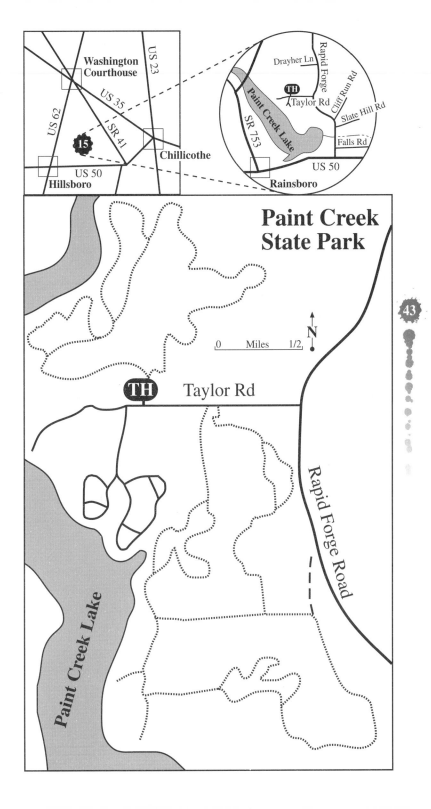

Washington
Courthouse

US 23

US 35

US 62

SR 41

15

US 50

Hillsboro

Chillicothe

Drayher Ln

Rapid Forge

Cliff Run Rd

TH

Taylor Rd

Slate Hill Rd

Paint Creek Lake

SR 753

Falls Rd

US 50

Rainsboro

Paint Creek
State Park

43

N

0   Miles   1/2

TH   Taylor Rd

Rapid Forge Road

Paint Creek Lake

Great Seal State Park

20 miles / Moderate - Challenging

Overview: True to its name this park has the hills which provided the inspiration for Ohio's State Seal. And hills there are. Traveling south on US 23, this is really the first decent change in topography you see after leaving Lake Erie's shore. The 20 miles of trail were built with horses or superhuman hikers in mind, so if you go be prepared to hike-a-bike.

Trail Description: Like Scioto Trail to the south there are some serious bomber trails here. If climbing for more than 5 minutes doesn't interest you then you should avoid Great Seal. No matter where you enter the system of trails you *will* wind up climbing. That is, until you hit a section too steep to climb, and then you'll be walking. Slowly. Uphill. Switchbacks mean nothing here, or anywhere else in Ohio, for that matter. One example: the nearly 500 foot climb on the 2 mile Sugarloaf Mountain Trail (yellow blazes). Only about a quarter mile of that is taken up by the climb, the rest is reasonable. The view is great in the autumn and the descent, on either side, is a rush of good singletrack if the horses haven't been by lately.

Most of the other trails are more of the same. Spring Run Trail is about the only level ground you'll find, with wide and rolling grassy trails. For a long outing try Shawnee Ridge (blue blazes) and you'll get to ride through some interesting rock formations. Watch for spur trails on the edge of the park as many of these head off to private property and are not marked as so. Makes it easy to get lost. Some riders have found themselves in downtown Chillicothe before figuring out that they were lost.

How To Get There: From almost any direction you'll approach this park from US 23. Basically, head towards Chillicothe and on to US 23. Just north of town is a sign for Great Seal State Park and Delano Road. Go east on Delano. You will cross railroad tracks then take a right on Marietta. The entrance to the park and the Sugarloaf Mountain trailhead is on the left. For Mt. Ives Trail continue south on Marietta and take a left on Rocky Road. From Rocky Road take a right on Lick Run Road. Parking and trailhead is just off the road.

Notes: Park @ 740-773-2726. Emergency @ 911. Trails heavily used by horses and hikers near the trailheads.

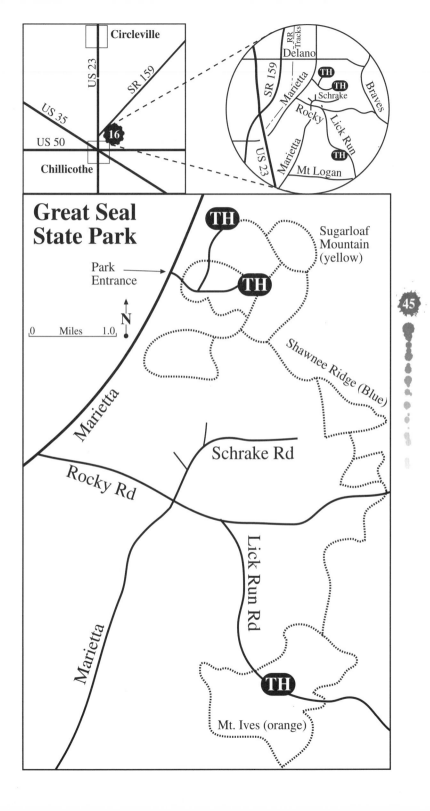

Circleville

US 23

SR 159

US 35

US 50

16

Chillicothe

RR Tracks

Delano

SR 159

Marietta

TH

TH

Schrake

Braves

Rocky

Lick Run

Marietta

Mt Logan

TH

Great Seal
State Park

TH

Sugarloaf
Mountain
(yellow)

Park
Entrance

N

0   Miles   1.0

Marietta

Shawnee Ridge (Blue)

Schrake Rd

Rocky Rd

Lick Run Rd

Marietta

45

TH

Mt. Ives (orange)

Tar Hollow State Park

2.6 miles / Easy - Moderate

Overview: This park is one of the unknown jewels in the state park system. Located in the 3rd largest state forest, Tar Hollow is the only legal spot where you can go two wheeling off road in famous Hocking County. The 2.6 mile loop combines flat fast singletrack and hilly technical riding, with a few stream crossings thrown in for good measure.

Trail Description: The Central Ohio Mountain Bike Organization helped Tar Hollow design and build the trail so you know it's made with bikers in mind. While the trail officially starts at the concessions area above the lake the real fun begins below the dam. Riding the loop clockwise, the trail east of the creek is relatively flat singletrack wrapping through hardwoods then pines. There are small 2 to 3 foot dips which have endo potential at speed.

Once you cross the creek heading west things get more technical and you will encounter big hills, offcamber climbs, and some fast descents. On the hillsides the vegetation is thick and lush providing a very tropical feel. The trail is well marked and a skilled rider can clear everything. A couple of laps will definitely get your blood pumping. This trail system will likely be expanded as COMBO has been invited back to continue its work. And there is a ton of potential.

How To Get There: From Columbus take US 23 south to SR 56 east in Circleville. Follow SR 56 to SR 180/SR 327 south through Adelphi. Stay on SR 327 for about 7 miles. You will see the park entrance on the right. Follow the road in and take the first left to park below the spillway or continue on FR 10 around the lake to the park's general store. From the south SR 327 can be accessed via US 50 just east of Chillicothe.

Notes: Park @ 740-887-4818. Emergency @ 911. Needs more trail open to bikes to make it worth a road trip.

You don't need mountains to have good mountain biking.

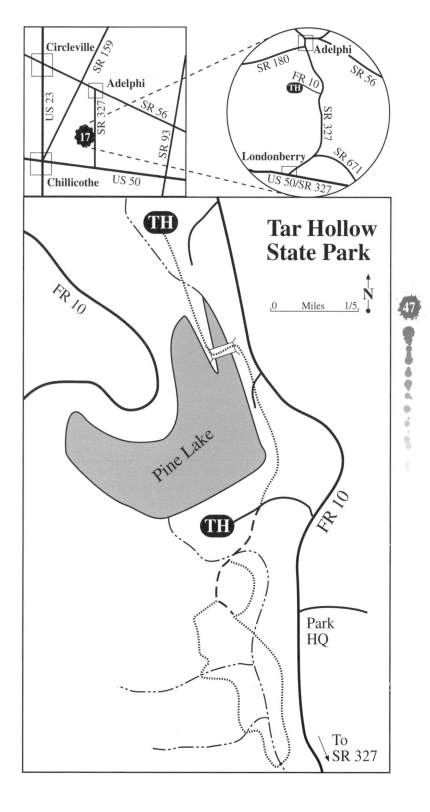

Circleville
SR 159
Adelphi
SR 56
US 23
SR 327
SR 93
17
Chillicothe US 50

Adelphi
SR 180
FR 10
TH
SR 56
SR 327
Londonberry
SR 671
US 50/SR 327

TH

Tar Hollow
State Park

FR 10

0   Miles   1/5

N

47

Pine Lake

TH

FR 10

Park
HQ

To
SR 327

Scioto Trail State Forest and State Park

40 miles / Easy - Moderate - Challenging

Overview: With a combination of gravel forest roads, bridle and hiking trails all open to mountain bikes, there is something here for everyone. This was the first State Forest to make its trails multiple use and while it has been a great success ODNR has yet to implement this policy elsewhere. There are huge hills and lots of potential when the trails are in good shape. However, expect some areas to be overgrown with briar or absolutely cratered by horses. Some are cherry, others are the pits. The main Buckeye Trail is generally well marked, well groomed, and well worth it. New singletrack trails are a big improvement, as are the new trail maps and location markers.

Trail Description: Lots to ride, with almost 40 miles of trails and 20 miles of gravel roads to connect it all together between the park and forest. A word of caution, if you don't like big hills don't ride here. The central and south area is most heavily used by mountain bikers. Expect beautiful scenery, with mature pines and lots of creek crossings to cool you down.

For a challenging loop starting below Stewart Lake (#45 on the map) and follow the Buckeye Trail east to Cemetery Trail. Make the detour up Cemetery Hill (#3) and check out one of Ohio's best mountain biking vistas. You can road ride back (at #10) or start working south using the new trail across Stoney Creek Road which follows along Hatfield Road/ FR 5. The South Ridge Trail is also great singletrack for an out-and-bike ride (#48 to 49). The northern bridle trails are poorly maintained so ride at your own risk.

For a less demanding riding there are a number of options. The trails surrounding Caldwell and Stewart Lakes have easy access from the campgrounds. Want to get further away from people? Try starting at access point #10 and ride north on Long Branch Trail. You will enjoy a couple of miles of level creekside riding before the trail starts to head uphill.

How To Get There: Scioto Trail is located just south of Chillicothe off US 23. From Columbus follow US 23 south and you will see the signs nine miles past Chillicothe. From Cincinnati take SR 32 east to US 23 north. Start looking for the signs just past Alma on the right. Once in the park there are several trailheads to choose from depending on the type of adventure you seek.

Notes: The Forest Service is using a new marking system at all trail intersections. These numbers do not correspond to mailage. Hosts an annual Family Mountain Bike Campout Weekend and races. Park @ 740-663-2125. Forest @ 740-663-2523. Emergency @ 911.

Horses have the right-of-way!!! If you see a horse STOP and DISMOUNT until they have passed. This is deadly serious as a spooked horse can kill its rider or even a mountain biker deity like yourself. Also, slow down for hikers and alert them to your presence with a big "Howdy!" One final word of caution: this State Forest is open to most forms of hunting. If you ride during the late fall wear bright colors and feel free to make lots of noise. Earth tones and silence may kill you.

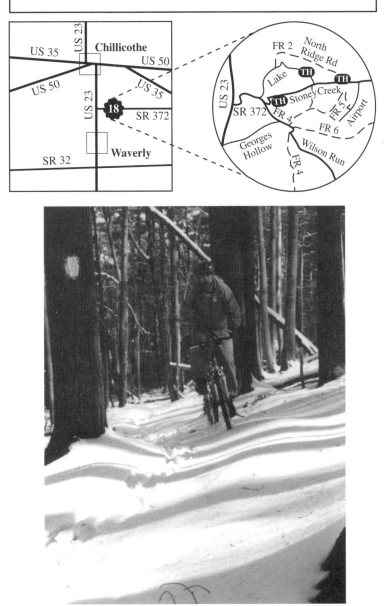

Winter riding at Scioto Trail State Park and Forest.

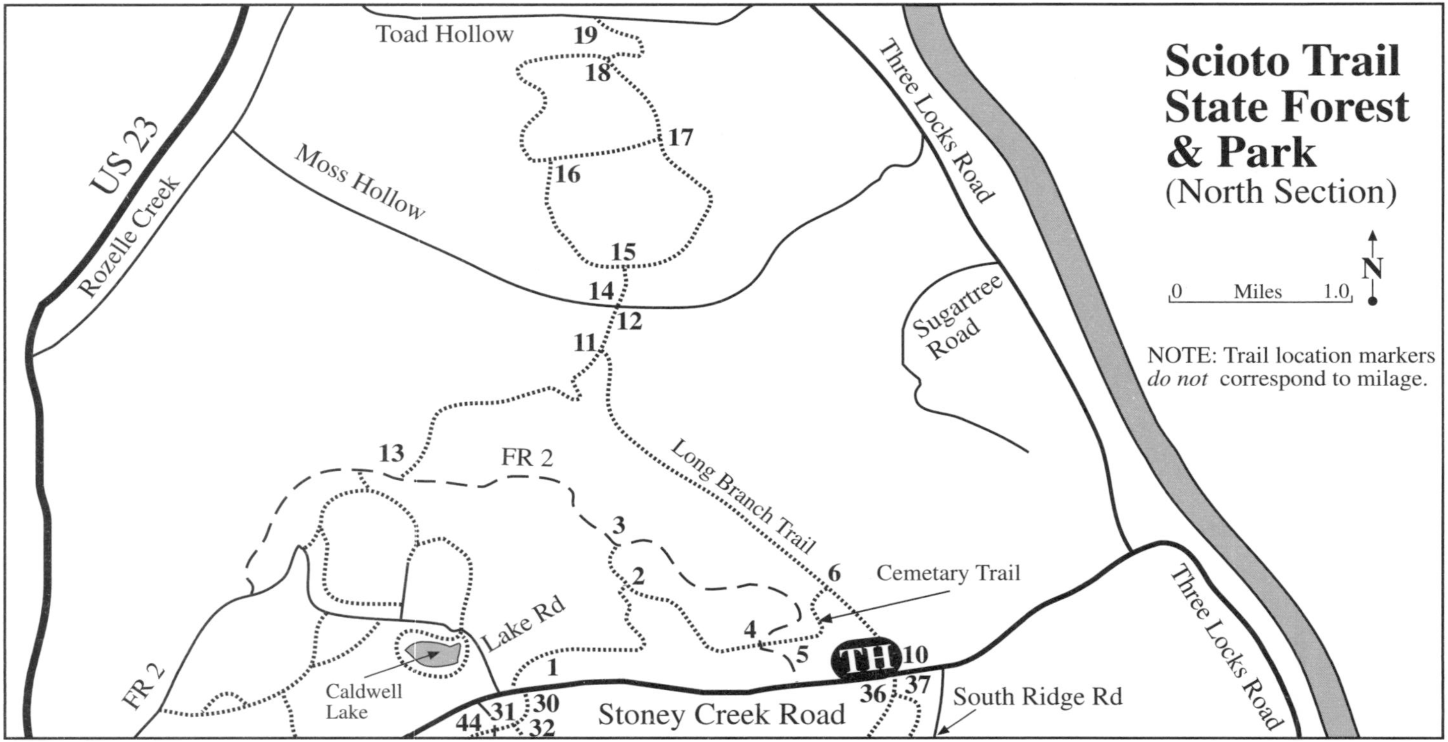

Scioto Trail State Forest & Park (North Section)

0 — Miles — 1.0

N

NOTE: Trail location markers *do not* correspond to milage.

50

Three Locks Road

Three Locks Road

Suwannee Road

US 23

Rozelle Creek

Toad Hollow

Moss Hollow

FR 2

FR 2

Long Branch Trail

Cemetery Trail

Lake Rd

Stoney Creek Road

South Ridge Rd

Caldwell Lake

TH

10
36 37
5
4
6
3
2
1
30
31 32
44
13
11
12
14
15
16
17
18
19

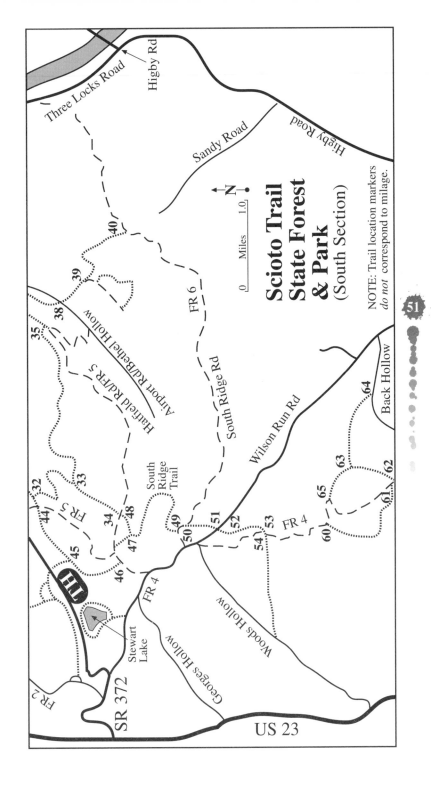

Scioto Trail State Forest & Park
(South Section)

NOTE: Trail location markers *do not* correspond to milage.

N

0   Miles   1.0

51

26 miles / Challenging

Overview: Located in southern Ohio, these Off-Road Vehicle (ORV) trails begin to resemble those of their southern neighbor, Kentucky. There is more rock, steeper hills, and a sandy-loam soil that is great when it's dry but erosive as hell when it's wet. It acts like sandpaper on any moving parts of your bike. Basically, all of them. The trails are composed of a maze of interconnected loops, gravel roads and jeep tracks. The roads come in handy for cutting a ride short when the water starts running low and the power grub is almost spent. At a minimum, take a full day to ride here as it's a big place and can get confusing with unmarked spur trails cut by ORVs.

Trail Description: There are 26 miles of trails, not including the jeep tracks, which radiate out from the parking area. Forest Road 105 bisects the area and is a constant reference point on almost every loop. Like the state's other ORV trails expect big climbs, long fast descents, and if it's wet, mud, mud, mud. If it has been a wet spring or autumn, and it seems they all are, you will begin to feel that more of the trail is under water than above it. Wait until summer and the trails are hard and fast. These trails have a much needed technical element not found in many other parts of the state: rocks. Lots of 'em. Big ones. Just waiting to hurt you. The trails are marked with difficulty ratings posted. Not for riders without a spirit of adventure because you *will* get lost.

How To Get There: Hanging Rock is located north of Ironton. From north or central Ohio travel south on US 23 out of Columbus. Follow this to Portsmouth then east on US 52 to Hanging Rock and SR 650 north. Follow SR 650 for about a mile to the Hanging Rock ORV sign and FR 105 on the left. The trailhead is 1 mile in on your right.

Notes: Trails closed December 15 - April 15. Forest @ 740-532-3223. Emergency @ 1-800-282-7777 or 740-532-3525 or 740-354-7566.

Riding in the Wayne, your public forest, is no longer free. You must purchase a daily ($5) or annual ($25) pass to do anything except walk around. Permits can be obtained at the District Office at 216 Columbus Road in Athens or your finer bike shops around the state. You should also tell them what you think about the program. Seems like we should get some singletrack of our own out of this investment. ORV Warning! These trails get intense use from ORV riders who are generally friendly to mountain bikers. When an ORV approaches, remember to move completely off the trail, if possible, maintaining a good line of sight. It has become customary using hand signals to sign the number in your group to the ORV riders so everyone will know what to expect. Summer riding is best as it takes the area a while to dry out in the spring and the ORVs churn up a lot of mud. Weekends are busiest. The trails are closed from December 15 to April 15 to reduce erosion. One final word of caution: this National Forest is open to most forms of hunting. If you ride during the late fall wear bright colors and feel free to make lots of noise. Earth tones and silence may kill you.

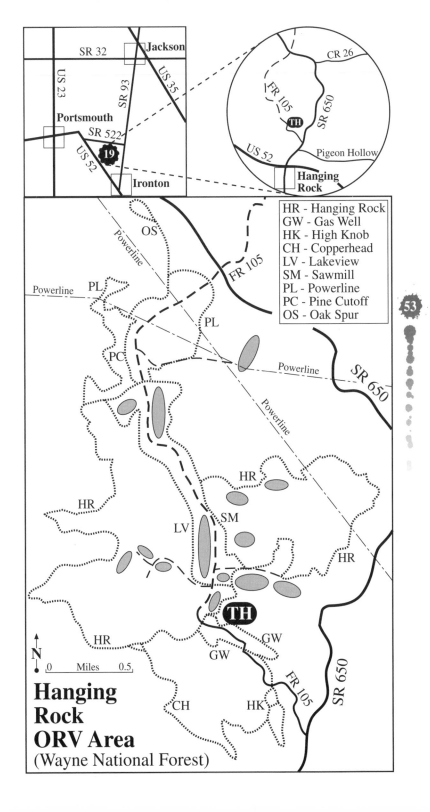

SR 32
Jackson
US 23
US 35
SR 93
Portsmouth
SR 522
US 52
19
Ironton

CR 26
FR 105
SR 650
TH
US 52
Pigeon Hollow
Hanging Rock

OS
FR 105
Powerline
Powerline
PL
PL
PC
Powerline
SR 650
Powerline

HR - Hanging Rock
GW - Gas Well
HK - High Knob
CH - Copperhead
LV - Lakeview
SM - Sawmill
PL - Powerline
PC - Pine Cutoff
OS - Oak Spur

53

HR
HR
SM
LV
HR
TH
GW
GW
HR
FR 105
SR 650
CH
HK

N
0   Miles   0.5

Hanging
Rock
ORV Area
(Wayne National Forest)

Pine Creek ORV Area, Wayne NF, Ironton Unit

20 miles / Challenging

Overview: Located in Southern Ohio, these Off-Road Vehicle (ORV) trails are on National Forest lands. The three trails which compose Pine Creek are not interconnecting loops, so riding here is an investment of time and energy. Also, finding the Lyra trailhead takes one into *not* the most mountain-biker-friendly looking part of Ohio. Don't expect too much beauty as this is an active coal mining region and these lands have experienced every type of abuse possible from grazing to plowing to clear-cutting to strip-mining. Welcome to your public lands and please don't drink the orange water.

Trail Description: The 20 miles of trail that compose Pine Creek create a rough upside down Y. Except for a small 2 mile loop just north of Wolcott Trailhead, the remainder of the trail is a straight shot from one point to the other. In theory, that is. Locals and careless ORVers have cut many illegal trails which can get you off course and lost fast. Remember, if it doesn't look official, it probably isn't. No loop means either riding out-and-back, setting up a shuttle, or creating a loop using the roads available. Other than the second option, you had better be in shape because you're in for a long haul. Expect big climbs, bomber downhills, and if it's wet, yep, you guessed it, mud. Try not to get that acid mine drainage water on your nice steel frame - bad things might happen.

How To Get There: Pine Creek is located south of Oak Hill. There are three trailheads with the most convenient being Telegraph Trailhead. From north or central Ohio follow US 23 south to US 35 east in Chillicothe. Take SR 32 west one mile to SR 93 south. Follow SR 93 into the Wayne Nation Forest. Look for CR 193 and a sign for Telegraph Trailhead on the right. The trailhead is 0.1 mile in on the left. From Cincinnati take SR 32 east to SR 93 south. From the east take SR 32 west to SR 93 south.

Notes: Trails closed December 15 - April 15. Forest @ 740-532-3223. Emergency @ 1-800-282-7777 or 740-532-3525 or 740-354-7566.

Riding in the Wayne, your public forest, is no longer free. You must purchase a daily ($5) or annual ($25) pass to do anything except walk around. Permits can be obtained at the District Office at 216 Columbus Road in Athens or your finer bike shops around the state. You should also tell them what you think about the program. Seems like we should get some singletrack of our own out of this investment. ORV Warning! These trails get intense use from ORV riders who are generally friendly to mountain bikers. When an ORV approaches, remember to move completely off the trail, if possible, maintaining a good line of sight. It has become customary using hand signals to sign the number in your group to the ORV riders so everyone will know what to expect. Summer riding is best as is takes the area a while to dry out in the spring and the ORVs churn up a lot of mud. Weekends are busiest. The trails are closed from December 15 to April 15 to reduce erosion. One final word of caution: this National Forest is open to most forms of hunting. If you ride during the late fall wear bright colors and feel free to make lots of noise. Earth tones and silence may kill you.

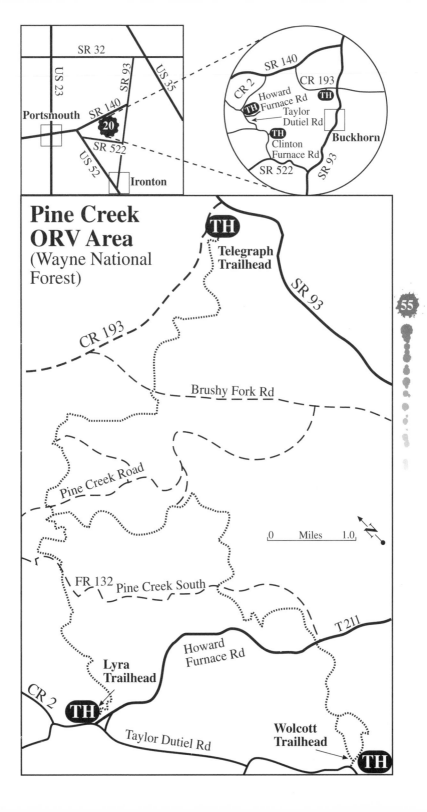

Pine Creek ORV Area
(Wayne National Forest)

SR 32
US 23
US 93
SR 93
US 35
SR 140
Portsmouth
20
SR 522
US 52
Ironton

SR 140
CR 2
CR 193
Howard Furnace Rd
TH
Taylor Dutiel Rd
TH
Clinton Furnace Rd
SR 522
SR 93
Buckhorn
TH

TH
Telegraph Trailhead

SR 93

CR 193

Brushy Fork Rd

Pine Creek Road

0   Miles   1.0

N

FR 132 Pine Creek South

T 211

Howard Furnace Rd

Lyra Trailhead

CR 2
TH

Taylor Dutiel Rd

Wolcott Trailhead
TH

55

Richland Furnace State Forest APV Area

7 miles / Moderate - Challenging

Overview: The Richland Furnace State Forest All-Purpose Vehicle (APV) Area is tucked in a beautiful forested valley between Chillicothe and Athens. The trails are developed for APVs but the area seems to get less use than the state's other APV areas. For you, the mountain biker, this means two things: 1) the trails are usually in good shape, and 2) you have less chance of getting run over. Expect big hills, fast descents, huge air, and a bit of technical riding. A good place to test which is in better shape: your body or your bike. The smart money is on your bike.

Trail Description: There are 7 miles of trails, with two main loops and two spur loops. There is only one way in and out, so it is almost impossible to get lost. Most trails are about 3 feet wide. Getting in involves a half-mile climb gaining 400 feet to warm you up. If you need motivation consider that on the way out you can fly down this puppy at 35+ mph! That may seem slow in your truck, but man it's blazing on a bike! Most of the riding is open and carefree but some of the descents require your full attention. A few of the steep climbs make you almost envy those loud motorheads but they are do-able if the ground is dry. Good luck if it's wet as this place has the slickest mud in Ohio. It's like riding on ice in August. the two main loops provice the best mountain biking. Worth a visit but you probably won't go back a second time.

How To Get There: Richland Furnace is located 24 miles east of Chillicothe. Take US 50 east to SR 327 south. Follow SR 327 for 10 miles to Loop Rd. (CR 32). Look for the Richland Furnace APV Area sign. Parking area and trailhead is 0.5 miles down Loop Road on the left.

Notes Seem to get less APV use than other state forests which means weekend riding is possible. However, weekday riding is still advisable to avoid getting run over. Trails closed December 1 to March 31. Forest @ 740-596-5781. Emergency @ 740-596-5781.

APV Warning! These trails get intense use from APV riders who are generally friendly to mountain bikers. When an APV approaches, remember to move completely off the trail, if possible, maintaining a good line of sight. It has become customary using hand signals to sign the number in your group to the APV riders so everyone will know what to expect. Summer riding is best as is takes the area a while to dry out in the spring and the APVs churn up a lot of mud. Weekends are busiest. The trails are closed from December 1 to March 31 to reduce erosion. One final word of caution: this state forest is open to most forms of hunting. If you ride during the late fall wear bright colors and feel free to make lots of noise. Earth tones and silence may kill you.

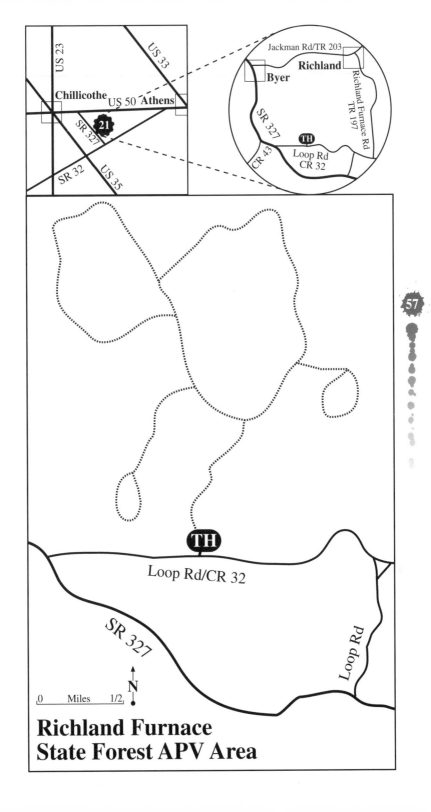

Richland Furnace
State Forest APV Area

US 23
US 33
Chillicothe
US 50 Athens
SR 327
21
SR 32 US 35

Jackman Rd/TR 203
Richland
Byer
Richland Furnace Rd
TR 197
SR 327
TH
CR 43
Loop Rd
CR 32

57

TH
Loop Rd/CR 32
SR 327
Loop Rd

0 Miles 1/2
N

Lake Hope State Park

3 miles / Easy - Moderate

Overview: This park features the 126 acre Lake Hope and is located inside Zaleski State Forest. Small hills covered with hardwoods make this a good place to catch the autumn colors in southern Ohio. The riding is not technical but can be fun and fast in places. If you are already in the neighborhood it's worth a look.

Trail Description: The short 3 mile Little Sandy Trail is officially sanctioned for mountain biking and shared with hikers. From the trailhead on Cabin Ridge Road, a 0.5 mile singletrack trail cuts through a mature forest. This short spur intersects 0.5 miles into Little Sandy Trail. Head right and the trail starts relatively flat, following a creek, until it rises out of the valley to connect with Cabin Ridge Road. Yes, you gain a little elevation with 220 feet of climbing. You can stay on the main trail for a more gradual climb out or take the first right you come to and grunt it out up a steeper climb. Both trails end at Cabin Ridge Road. Using the road one can make a nice loop back to the trailhead. Another option is to ride the road up and cruise down the trail. Duh.

How To Get There: Lake Hope is located off SR 278 fifteen miles due east of Athens. From the east follow SR 278 south from US 33 in Nelsonville or SR 56 from Athens. You will pass the first two park entrances on the right and the backpacking parking lot on the left before you come to Cabin Ridge Road. Turn right on Cabin Ridge Road and the mountain bike trailhead and parking is immediately on your left. From the west and US 50 follow SR 278 north and turn in the first main entrance on the left.

Notes: Park @ 740-596-4938. Emergency @ 740-596-9911 or 740-596-5255.

A sunny day, a dry trail, and no APVs in sight.

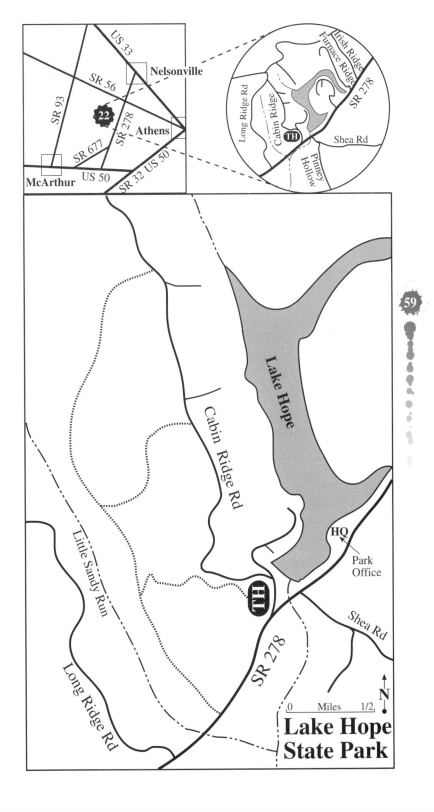

US 33
Nelsonville
SR 56
SR 93
22
SR 278
Athens
SR 677
McArthur
US 50
SR 32 US 50

Irish Ridge
Furnace Ridge
Long Ridge Rd
Cabin Ridge
TH
SR 278
Shea Rd
Pinney Hollow

Cabin Ridge Rd

Lake Hope

Little Sandy Run

HQ
Park Office

TH

Shea Rd

SR 278

Long Ridge Rd

59

0   Miles   1/2

N

Lake Hope
State Park

Monday Creek ORV Area, Wayne NF, Athens Unit

72 miles / Challenging

Overview: While these trails are often referred to as Dorr Run, it is actually only one of several located in the Athens Unit of the Wayne National Forest. The official name is the Monday Creek Off-Road Vehicle (ORV) Area which total 72 miles. This means the trails are generally very wide, with no true singletrack. However, the hills are as big as they come in Ohio which means you can get blazing speed, tons of air, and banked corners beg for attention as you ride through at angles you never thought possible! There is something for everyone here. Lots of mud in the spring.

Trail Description: *Dorr Run Loop* - Being accessible from SR 33, this trail is best known. While called a loop, it is actually a number of loops which make up the majority of trail in Monday Creek. You will find some of the most challenging mountain biking here with an unending series of hills, long winding climbs, killer descents, and tons of places to get air. Spur trails crop up like weeds and it's easy to get lost so it is best to discover Dorr Run a small section at a time. Many riders have had to find their way out muddy, tired, and hungry - don't be one of them.

Snake Hollow - Access is from Dorr Run Loop or CR 24. Creates about a 4 mile loop if ridden in from CR 24 parking area. Similar trails to Dorr Run and you have a good chance of seeing lots of ORVs.

Long Ridge - Access is from SR 78 to FR 758. This trail does not get as much use, as it is not tied directly into the other trails. Here you can ride a series of loops for about 7 miles on some of the more technical riding in Monday Creek. This area has two of the best downhill rides in the Wayne. Hey, you can finally justify that full suspension bike!

Main Corridor - Multiple access points. Stretches from Snake Hollow north to New Straitsville Trailhead. Covers the entire spectrum of riding in Wayne, from easy to difficult, flat to seemingly vertical. Mostly intermediate level riding, however, it is a long straight shot, so whatever distance you cover, you also have to ride back. Two options, set up a shuttle at New Straitsville and either Snake Hollow or Dorr Run, or, ride the forest service roads back. Main Corridor provides some of the best views of the rolling hills and fall colors.

New Straitsville - Access is from SR 595. This is the north end of the Main Corridor Trail and contains a 3 mile loop. Any level of rider can do this section but it is especially good for beginners and people addicted to air. If taken clockwise, there is an extended series of jumps on a quarter-mile downhill. We're talking frequent flier miles here. Enjoy!

How To Get There: The Athens Unit of the Wayne National Forest is located just off US 33 north of Nelsonville. Follow the access notes above and look for the access signs.

Notes: Trails closed December 15 - April 15. Don't even think about riding here during gun deer hunting season! Forest @ 740-592-6644. Emergency @ 740-593-6633 or 740-385-2131 or 740-342-4123.

Riding in the Wayne, your public forest, is no longer free. You must purchase a daily ($5) or annual ($25) pass to do anything except walk around. Permits can be obtained at the District Office at 216 Columbus Road in Athens or your finer bike shops around the state. You should also tell them what you think about the program. Seems like we should get some singletrack of our own out of this investment. ORV Warning! These trails get intense use from ORV riders who are generally friendly to mountain bikers. When an ORV approaches, remember to move completely off the trail, if possible, maintaining a good line of sight. It has become customary using hand signals to sign the number in your group to the ORV riders so everyone will know what to expect. Summer riding is best as is takes the area a while to dry out in the spring and the ORVs churn up a lot of mud. Weekends are busiest. The trails are closed from December 15 to April 15 to reduce erosion. One final word of caution: this national forest is open to most forms of hunting. If you ride during the late fall wear bright colors and feel free to make lots of noise. Earth tones and silence may kill you.

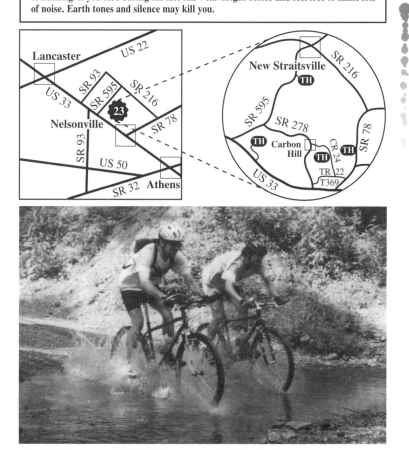

Cooling down mountain biker style.

61

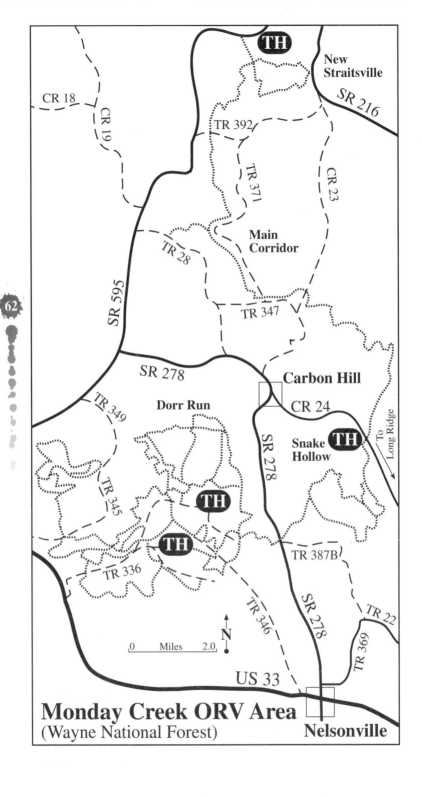

Monday Creek ORV Area
(Wayne National Forest)

CR 18

CR 19

TH

New Straitsville

SR 216

TR 392

TR 371

CR 23

Main Corridor

TR 28

SR 595

TR 347

SR 278

Carbon Hill

CR 24

To Long Ridge

TR 349

Dorr Run

Snake Hollow

TH

TR 345

SR 278

TH

TH

TR 336

TR 387B

TR 346

SR 278

TR 22

TR 369

N

0   Miles   2.0

US 33

Nelsonville

62

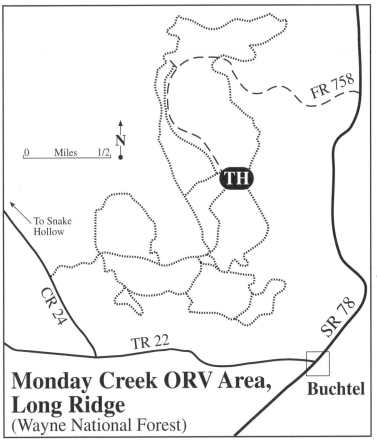

FR 758

N

0   Miles   1/2

TH

To Snake
Hollow

CR 24

TR 22

SR 78

Buchtel

Monday Creek ORV Area,
Long Ridge
(Wayne National Forest)

Ohio's "Little Utah", Perry State Forest APV Area.

Denison University Biological Reserve

4 miles / Easy

Overview: The Denison Reserve's 350 acres is managed for high biological diversity, *not* recreation. The fact that they allow mountain biking shows their understanding of the compatibility of a sound ecosystem and recreational use. It's a testament to good land management. Here you will find some nice trails winding through open meadows, old hardwoods, and planted pines. Quite diverse scenery and a nice local resource for beginning riders.

Trail Description: This is a great place for inexperienced riders to pick up some skills. There are no real technical aspects except for sharp turns, which only become a gamble at higher speeds. You'll also find out if you're up to the climbs that come with mountain biking. There are a few big hills which will be a challenge to the novice rider and pure fun for those with more experience.

The trail system's 4 miles are very well maintained and you should expect to encounter hikers and trail runners, so be prepared to yield. You'll find some nice open field riding along with a pine tree plantation that is very cool to take a breather in. Wildlife watching is great with ponds, streams, open fields and lots of bird boxes. Do not disturb the plants, animals, or ongoing experiments. So boys and girls, ride responsibly and show this can work.

How To Get There: From Columbus take SR 161 east to Granville. Pay attention and you can exit Newark-Granville Road into downtown. If you miss it take exit SR 37 and go north into downtown then right on Newark-Granville and follow the signs for SR 166 north. The entrance to the reserve is just north of town on the right. From the south and I-70 follow SR 37 north to Granville.

Notes: Subject to seasonal closure. Not all the trails in the Reserve are open to bikes and closed trails are marked as so. Good local resource but not worth a road trip. Emergency @ 911.

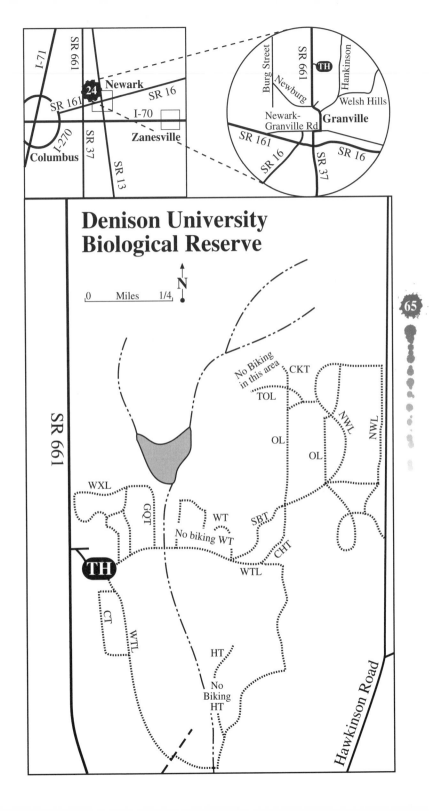

Denison University Biological Reserve

N

0   Miles   1/4

SR 661

No Biking in this area

CKT

TOL

OL

NWL

NWL

OL

WXL

GQT

WT

SBT

No biking WT

CHT

WTL

TH

CT

WTL

HT

No Biking HT

Hawkinson Road

I-71
SR 661
SR 161
I-270
Columbus
24
Newark
SR 16
I-70
Zanesville
SR 37
SR 13

Burg Street
Newburg
SR 661
TH
Hankinson
Welsh Hills
Newark-Granville Rd
Granville
SR 161
SR 16
SR 37
SR 16

65

Perry State Forest
APV Area

13 miles / Moderate - Challenging

Overview: These trails are developed for All-Purpose Vehicles (APVs) and they are heavily used by motorcross riders. What does this mean to you? Some of them can get pretty extreme and you are almost guaranteed to find something you cannot ride. You are also guaranteed to find great jumps, screamin' steep downhills, serious moguls, and mud. This place is still pretty much a secret to most mountain bikers.

Trail Description: Officially, there are 13 miles of developed trails in the Perry APV Area. The forest service has designated and marked eight color-coded trails. Maintenance is not as good as that of other state forests APV areas which makes these trails more singletrack in nature. The trails east of the parking area wind around and through many bare, unrecovered mined slopes. This is kind of a lunar landscape/motorcross playland. Do you really have eight inches of travel? Find out for sure! This is where you will spend the majority of your time in Perry. The rest of the area is a combination of forested trails with big hills, rutted descents, and potentially a lot of mud. Don't fall though, this place has the smelliest mud in the state. And while that crystal clear water in the acid mine drainage ponds may look refreshing, you might want to wait and clean your bike at home.

How To Get There: The Perry State Forest APV trailhead is located off SR 345 north of New Lexington. From the west follow I-70 east to SR 13 south. Follow SR 13 to New Lexington and SR 345 north. You will see the sign for the APV trails just past the Forest Headquarters. Turn left on TR 154 and follow this to the parking area 0.6 miles in. Trailheads are at the end of the parking area and north 0.1 mile further down TR 154.

Notes: Trails closed December 1 to March 31. Forest @ 740-674-4035. Emergency @ 911.

APV Warning! These trails get intense use from APV riders who are generally friendly to mountain bikers. When an APV approaches, remember to move completely off the trail, if possible, maintaining a good line of sight. It has become customary using hand signals to sign the number in your group to the APV riders so everyone will know what to expect. Summer riding is best as is takes the area a while to dry out in the spring and the APVs churn up a lot of mud. Weekends are busiest. The trails are closed from December 1 to March 31 to reduce erosion. One final word of caution: this state forest is open to most forms of hunting. If you ride during the late fall wear bright colors and feel free to make lots of noise. Earth tones and silence may kill you.

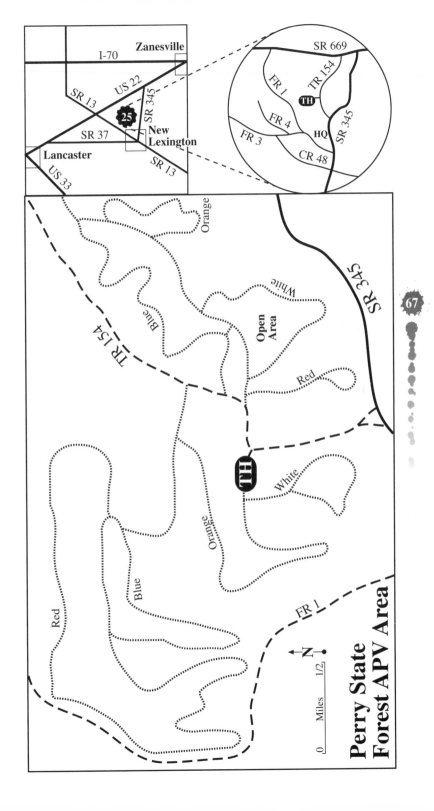

Perry State
Forest APV Area

67

Zanesville Velo-Z

5 miles / Moderate - Challenging

Overview: Fun, Fun, Fun! Located an hour east of Columbus, this trail is on private property and hosts a great series of summer races. It is a fast track for riders who love long descents without lots of technical junk getting in the way of their speed, and long climbs to drop all those downhill speed demons. Largely singletrack with some old logging roads that have almost reverted back to nature, this well planned 5 mile loop winds through a young, mixed forest. A fun place to enter the racing world.

Trail Description: This is about a 5 mile loop with lots of big hills, switchbacks, and a small creek-crossing or two. When it's dry it's fast and fun. And when it's wet, well, it doesn't slow down much then either. None of the hills are too steep to climb or descend for the experienced rider. A good course to race with lots of opportunity to pass or be passed. You will leave this ride satisfied! And if you haven't been back in a while, the owner has changed things up, adding some new technical trail. A challenge unique to this ride is going from a dark forest path into blinding sunlight then back into the shadows at speed. Even if you know the trail those milliseconds of riding blind are a real scare.

How To Get There: As the name implies the Zanesville Velo-Z is located just south of Zanesville off I-70. Head into Zanesville and follow SR 60 south through town and Duncan Falls. The driveway is not marked, so be looking for where the road has been cut into the hillside on the left and rock is exposed. Just as the rock ends there will be an unmarked gravel driveway on the left heading uphill. Take the drive past a house on the left and a huge red barn on the right until the road ends in a grass field at the top of the hill. A sign and payment box marks the trailhead. Now enjoy the view and don't forget to respect the land.

Notes: This is a private property Pay-To-Ride trail for experienced riders. Currently $5/day or $40/year with payment at trailhead. Money goes to charity so don't be a tightwad. Only racers are allowed to ride on race days so check your calendar before heading out. Better yet, race and support this great ride. If you don't like these rules then go ride somewhere else. Contact Tom Hayes @ 740-674-4297 for a race schedule. Emergency @ 911.

Map labels: SR 60, Zanesville, I-70, US 22, **Lancaster**, US 33, **26**, SR 60, I-77

Zanesville, I-70, SR 146, US 22, **Duncan Falls**, Rock Cliff, Muskingum River, SR 555, SR 60, Unpaved Drive, **TH**

Autumn colors at Fifty Springs Trail, Ceasar Creek State Park.

Marietta Unit, Wayne National Forest

82 miles / Challenging

Overview: Finally, there is a place in the Wayne National Forest where you can ride your bike without getting run over by an ORV! The Marietta Unit, bordering the Ohio River in far southeast Ohio, has eight hiking trails recently opening to mountain bikes. Forty-one miles of trail are split among seven loops and out-and-back rides. The North Country Trail adds another 41 miles open to bikes. This part of Ohio is very rugged and rocky. As Ohio's trail builders have never been very sympathetic to bikers, often heading straight up hillsides, expect some grueling climbs and quick elevation changes of hundreds of feet. Not for the timid. These trails are shared with hikers so remember to announce your presence and yield when appropriate.

Trail Description: *Ohio View Trail* is a 7 mile point to point ride. A shuttle can be set up starting at SR 260 and making a dramatic downhill ride to SR 7 and the Ohio River. There is also a 3.5 mile connector trail to the North Country Trail at Archers Fork.

Scenic River Trail is a 5.5 mile loop with some overlap at both ends of the trail. Starting at Leith Run Recreation Area on SR 7 the trail climbs out of the Ohio River Valley to rock bluffs overlooking the river. The other trailhead is located on CR 9.

Covered Bridge Trail is a 8 mile point-to-point ride through the hills above the Little Muskingum River. Both trailheads are located off SR 26 and feature historic 100 year old covered bridges. There is also a 3 mile connecter trail to the North Country Trail at Archers Fork.

Archers Fork Trail is a rugged 9.5 mile loop. It features numerous rock outcroppings and a sandstone rock bridge. The trail spans the bridge which is 51 feet long, 16 feet thick, and 39 feet above the ground. It's not Arches National Monument, but not bad for Ohio. Connector trails lead to Covered Bridge Trail to the west and Ohio View Trail to the east. Best access is from SR 260 to the north.

Lamping Homestead Trail has two loops of 1.8 and 3.2 miles. Located further north off of SR 26 this trail is not connected to the rest of the system and isn't as extreme as the rest of the trails in the Marietta Unit. See the inset map.

North Country Trail is a 41 mile section of a National Scenic Trail which is to eventually span 7 states and 3200 miles. This trail can be divided up into 8 sections: Lane Farm to Bear Run Road - 8.7 miles, Bear Run to

Scenic River Trail - 9.4 miles, Scenic River Trail to Archers Fork Trail - 2.7 miles, Archers Fork Trail to SR 260 - 1.8 miles, SR 260 to Wilson Run Road - 3.0 miles, Wilson Road to Knowlton Connector Trail - 5.7 miles, Knowlton Connector Trail to Ring Mill 3.0 miles. Point-to-point possibilities abound so set up a shuttle and explore. Just to let you know, the North Country Trail Assocation wants to ban bikes from as much of the trail as possible. Can't we all just get along?

How To Get There: Many of these roads are unpaved, poorly marked, or have local names which differ from what is listed on state maps. Be patient and have a full tank of gas. See trail description for trailhead location.

Notes: Trails closed December 15 to April 15. Don't even think about riding here during gun deer hunting season! Forest @ 740-373-9055. Emergency @ 740-373-2833. Seeking volunteers for trail maintenance.

Riding in the Wayne, your public forest, is no longer free. You must purchase a daily ($5) or annual ($25) pass to do anything except walk around. Permits can be obtained at the District Office at 216 Columbus Road in Athens or your finer bike shops around the state. You should also tell them what you think about the program. Seems like we should get some singletrack of our own out of this investment. The trails are closed from December 15 to April 15 to reduce erosion. One final word of caution: this national forest is open to most forms of hunting. If you ride during the late fall wear bright colors and feel free to make lots of noise. Earth tones and silence may kill you.

IMBA State Rep meeting. Working to get more trails opened.

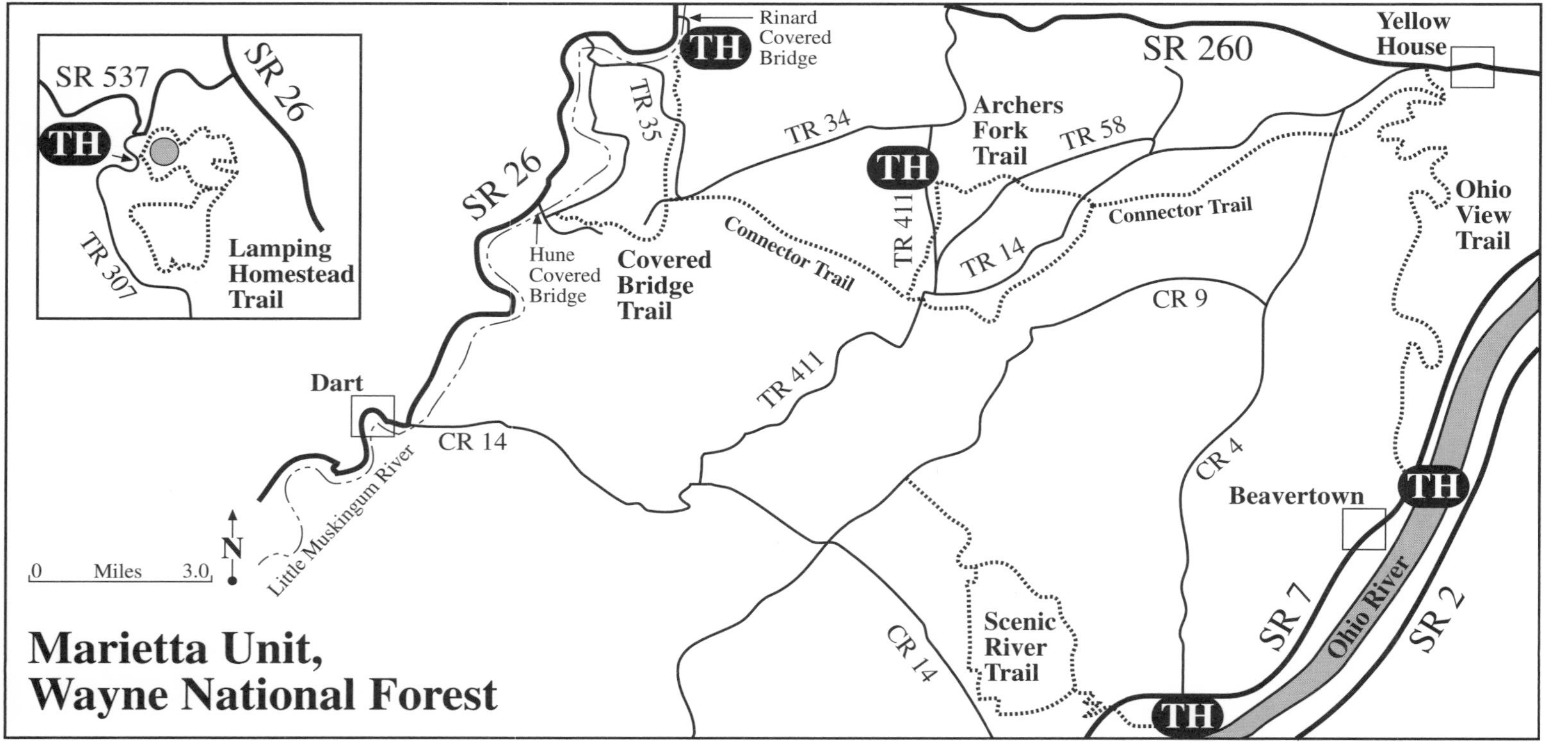

Marietta Unit,
Wayne National Forest

72

Yellow House

Ohio View Trail

SR 2

Ohio River

SR 7

Beavertown

CR 4

SR 260

Connector Trail

CR 9

TR 58

TR 14

Archers Fork Trail

Scenic River Trail

CR 14

TH

TR 411

TR 34

Connector Trail

TR 411

Rinard Covered Bridge

TH

TR 35

Covered Bridge Trail

Hune Covered Bridge

SR 26

CR 14

Dart

Little Muskingum River

SR 26

SR 537

Lamping Homestead Trail

TR 307

TH

N

0   Miles   3.0

Not a bike mechanic yet? Keep riding, you will be.

Mickey's Mountain

15 miles / Moderate - Challenging

Overview: Located just 27 miles from Wheeling, West Virginia, Mickey's has it all for racers! Crosscountry, dual slalom, downhill, hill climb and trials. They even have non-competitive night rides. Riding crosscountry you will find big hills, well-groomed singletrack, and a few creek crossings, on marked trails. While it is a long haul from most of Ohio, it is a good haul once you are there. Many racers say if you can win here, you can win anywhere. It's also one of the only spots in Ohio where you can watch national club teams race.

Trail Description: Two main loops compose the crosscountry trails with all racers, beginner through expert, riding the same track for the first mile or so. After the split, sport and expert racers follow a loop of 5-6 miles composed of fast singletrack hugging the sides of various hills with big, but do-able, climbs. Most trails are surprisingly compact and relatively mud-free. It's not the most technical course but instead very fast, allowing the rider no time to recover. If you're not in shape, you'll know it soon enough.

The beginner loop is shorter with fewer changes in elevation, but still full of good singletrack. At times it is even more technical in nature than the advanced loop, with more trees crowding the off-camber trail just waiting to rip the handlebar from your grasp. Almost all of the open field riding has been eliminated, replaced with fast wooded singletrack. Having a lot of land to work with, trail routes change frequently but are well marked.

The dual slalom course is the only one of its kind in Ohio and not to be missed. With banked turns and a double jump this course dismounts its share of riders. There is an advanced and beginner slalom on the same hillside so you can build your skills.

A 1000+ foot downhill course has been added and provides a whole new element of danger and spectator pleasure. Full suspension is the rule here. And you're crazy if you think hitting that hay bail will be a soft landing. Open for races only.

And for you masochists a marked hill climb course. They even left a few downed logs to keep you from getting cocky.

Trials riders also have a variety of logs, junked cars, and obstacles to clamber over. Makes bunny-hopping on that park bench childs play.

How To Get There: Mickey's Mountain is located just north of Hopedale off US 22. From the west take I-70 east to I-77 north. Continue east on US 22 to Hopedale. Exit at Hopedale and go north on CR 4 until you cross over 4 sets of railroad tracks and come to a stop sign. Go left at the stop sign on CR 46 for 0.5 miles. Look for Ford Road (CR 170), a dead-end road on the right, just before a green house. Follow this up to the end and park in the field to the right. You will see the race check-in shed and trailhead.

Notes: This is a private property Pay-To-Ride trail. Currently $5/day. Camping $5/day. Winter access requires positive confirmation of approval to ride. Call ahead to 740-946-5631 and leave a message. You must sign in and out at trailhead. Only racers are allowed to ride on race days so check your calendar before heading out. Better yet, race and support a professional mountain biking scene in Ohio. If you don't like the rules then go ride somewhere else. Mickeys @ 740-946-5631 or email mickeys@eohio.net. Emergency @ 740-946-5631 (Mickeys) or 740-942-2197 (sheriff).

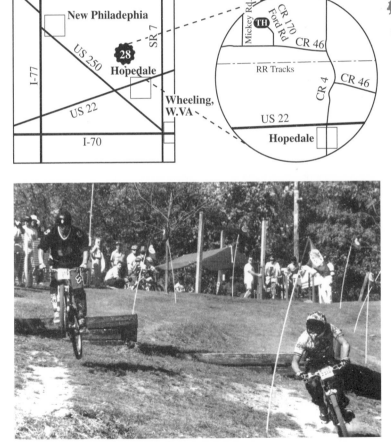

The dual slalom at Mickey's Mounain.

Jefferson Lake State Park

22 miles / Moderate

Overview: The big hills of eastern Ohio have provided great hiking, horse riding and backpacking for years. Finally Ohio's mountain bikers can take advantage of them. Well, sort of... Jefferson Lake's trails were largely designed with four legged animals in mind. Many go in two directions only - up or down. So get ready to hike-a-bike if you pick the wrong loop. On the bright side, pick the right trails and you get good rolling track, moderate climbs, and white knuckle descents.

Trail Description: With 22 miles of trail there's some good riding at every level. However, some of the newer tracks are a good example of why bulldozers shouldn't be used to cut trail for bikers, hikers and horses. Cheifly, bulldozers can easily go up hills the aforementioned animals cannot. And while it's probably quicker and cheaper to build, it's just no fun to ride. Skip Logans Trail altogether unless you enjoy mud, horse poop, and riding with your mouth closed.

Fortunately, not all of the new trail is unrideable, and the loop added just across from the end of the Trillium Trail has a strong climb, nice rolling crest and then a long fast descent. You can make a good 6 mile loop of it by starting at the Lakeside Trail and continuing down Trillium, up to the parking area, then across to the last section of Logan's. Backtrack to the lake on Trillium. Lakeside Trail is also a good level loop for a relaxing ride. However, whenever you ride these trails be prepared to get muddy. A number of them get right down in creek beds.

This would be a good place to camp and ride when racing at Mickey's Mountain which is only about 30 minutes away. Keep in mind this is rural Ohio and barking dogs on local farms make it sound like you're sleeping in a Tiajuana slum. Go figure.

How To Get There: From Cleveland/Akron take I-77 south to Canton. In south Canton go east on US 30 then south on SR 43. About 3 miles after you pass East Springfield you will see signs for Park Road, CR 54. Turn left and follow it to the park. At the park you will see the lake on your left. This is a good place to park and hit multiple trailheads from the beach area. From the south follow I-77 north to US 22 east and SR 43. Go west on SR 43. Park Road will be on your right just past Richmond.

Notes: Not a smart place to ride during hunting season. Camouflage bow hunters are everywhere. It's kind of unnerving. Park @ 740-765-4459. Emergency @ 911.

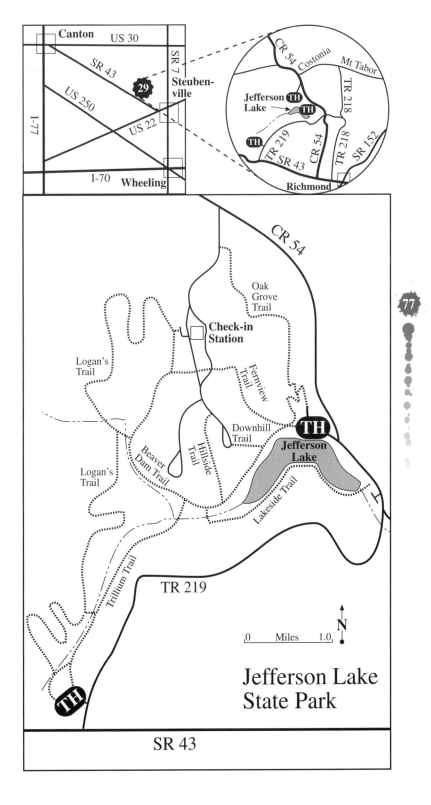

Canton
US 30
SR 43
SR 7
29
Steuben-
ville
US 250
I-77
US 22
I-70
Wheeling

CR 54
Costonia
Mt Tabor
Jefferson
Lake
TH
TH
TR 218
TH
TR 219
SR 43
CR 54
TR 218
SR 152
Richmond

CR 54
Oak
Grove
Trail
Check-in
Station
Fernview
Trail
Logan's
Trail
Downhill
Trail
Beaver
Dam
Trail
Hillside
Trail
Jefferson
Lake
TH
Logan's
Trail
Lakeside Trail
Trillium Trail
TR 219
0   Miles   1.0
N
TH
Jefferson Lake
State Park
SR 43

77

Beaver Creek State Park

8 miles / Moderate - Challenging

Overview: Beautiful trails in a beautiful state park, this is *the* ride of eastern Ohio. The trails follow the scenic Little Beaver Creek Valley, providing some of the nicest views you can get on knobby tires in Ohio. They are also a challenge. Spend too much time looking at all that beauty and you will likely wind up airborne and your landing will not be soft. It will be rock. A much needed change to the usual Ohio mud.

Trail Description: Beaver Creek has three trails open to mountain bikes and they are each unique. The Pine Ridge trail is a short 1 mile loop through a pine forest. Not much to see there. Now, if you really want to get someone new addicted to mountain biking, take them up the 2.2 mile Dogwood Trail. After a short rocky entrance, the trail follows Little Beaver Creek, rolling gently along with a beautiful view. It then begins a long climb out of the valley and the family may want to turn around. Near the top you can continue up to the Leslie Road camping area or descend on the rockiest trail in any state park. Make sure your dental insurance is paid before going down. Starting in the opposite direction the hike-a-bike sucks, but the ride down is long, sweeping, and flows like water. Do not attempt this climb if you have a 30 pound cruiser. It will kill you. Better yet, park at the top.

The Vondergreen Trail and Gretchen's Lock Trail provide a 4.5 mile out-and-back ride that should not be missed, and should be repeated often. You can start creekside just below the bridge and ride through lots of rocks, or start just down the road a bit where the trail takes a more lung-burning approach. You will follow fast singletrack along Little Beaver Creek until you see the turn for Gretchen's Lock Trail. It is marked "No horses." Head uphill and out of the valley. If you find yourself practically in the creek hiking your bike over rocks, you've missed the turnoff. The trail is about 250 feet above you on the left. At the turn you'll head up and, after reaching the top, follow a great singletrack which weaves in and out of trees offering an occasional view of the creek far below. A rocky switchback trail descends down to the creek, crossing the path of a number of horse trails. Stay off these trails. Once at the end turn around and go back!

How To Get There: From Cleveland take I-80 east to I-76 east. Just south of Youngstown exit I-76 to SR 7 south. After about 15 miles you can take a left on Carlisle or look for the park signs at Bell School Road. Recommend parking at the park HQ on Echo Dell Road where there are multiple access points. From the south or west follow I-70 east to SR 7 north.

Notes: Well worth the drive from Northeast Ohio. Trails closed during deer gun and muzzleloader hunting season. Park @ 330-385-3091. Emergency @ 911 or 330-385-3091.

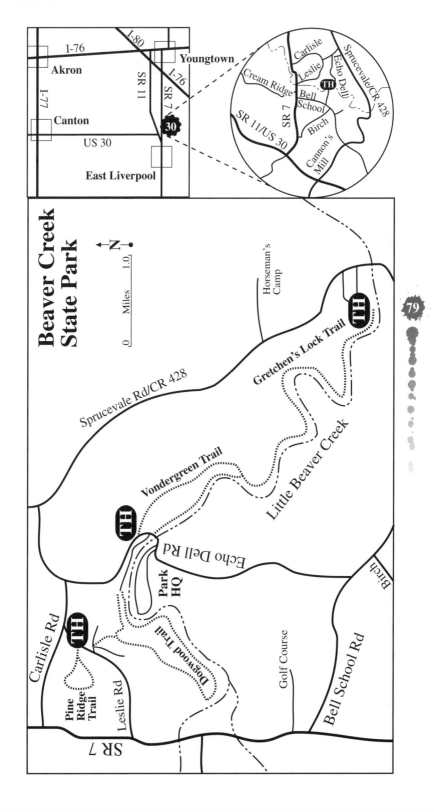

Beaver Creek State Park

N

Miles
0   1.0

79

Sprucevale Rd/CR 428

Gretchen's Lock Trail

Horseman's Camp

Vondergreen Trail

Little Beaver Creek

Echo Dell Rd

Park HQ

Dogwood Trail

Carlisle Rd

Pine Ridge Trail

Leslie Rd

Golf Course

Birch

Bell School Rd

SR 7

I-76

I-80

Akron

Youngtown

SR 11

I-77

I-76

SR 7

Canton

US 30

30

East Liverpool

Carlisle

Leslie

Echo Dell

Sprucevale/CR 428

Cream Ridge

Bell School

SR 7

Birch

SR 11/US 30

Cannon's Mill

TH

Mohican Wilderness Center

3 miles / Moderate - Challenging

Overview: Big climbs, fast descents, 90% singletrack, all cut for mountain bike racing! Need I say more? Okay, wooded, sometimes rocky, always fun. After riding this course, not only will you want to race, you will be convinced you can win.

Trail Description: This 3 mile loop is on private property at the Mohican Wilderness Center. A clockwise loop, the beginning is a grueling hill of singletrack, never steep enough to give you an excuse to dismount, yet never letting up until you are on top. At the top you hit an open field, duck into some short singletrack, then back into the field. Put it in your big ring, stand up, crank hard, and make some time. Take a right down the short stretch of gravel road then make a right back into the singletrack as you fly downhill. The downhill has tight turns, logs, rocks, a few quick dips, and even a little water. It's bliss! Then you are back at the start to do it all over again.

How To Get There: Mohican Wilderness Center is southeast of Mansfield. Easiest access is from SR 3, just south of Loundonville and north of SR 97. From SR 3 take County Road 3175, Wally Road, south. The trailhead is approximately 10 miles down on the right, just past the camping and signs for Mohican Wilderness Center. Drive up the big grass hill on the right or park in the field on the left side of the road. The trailhead is at the far end of the clearing in the pine trees.

Notes: This a is private property trail. Lots of camping in the area. Hosts Mohican Wilderness Race series. Call Knox County Visitors Bureau @ 1-800-837-5282 or 614-599-0078 for race dates. Emergency @ 911.

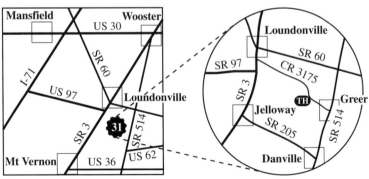

Vulture's Knob

7 miles / Moderate - Challenging

Overview: Simply put, this is the most technical trail in Ohio. And not surprisingly, it is located on private property, and has been cut with the serious mountain biker in mind. The original course is composed of a short, intense loop though wooded valleys, an old quarry, grassy hillsides and a small pine tree plantation. Definitely a trail for technical freaks. A second loop follows Killbuck Creek and its adjacent hillsides. More open than the original trail, technical surprises like the Broken Willow still await. Ohio's closest thing to riding in a Mountain Dew commercial.

Trail Description: Dr. Knob continues to add new elements to the main singletrack loop increasing its length to over 3 miles. Expect lots of short steep singletrack with little room for error. There are few long climbs to drop your friends and competitors on - this place is short, tight, and sweet with the longest straight run being the Power Line. Let go of the brakes and enjoy. Every downhill ends in a turn just sharp enough to kill your speed, followed by a pitched climb to destroy your remaining spirit. The numerous log bridges have became the stuff of legends. Don't let them psych you out or you'll be swimming in the Gold Fish Bowl.

A second loop known as Killbuck Run adds another 3 plus miles and features a lot of flat twisting singletrack through a creek bottom. Subject to flooding the trails are expanding towards the drier hillsides on the east. Expect more track to be added in the near future. The trail is well marked and hosts a fun, competitive race series and Ohio's only 24 hour race.

How To Get There: Vulture's Knob is located west of Wooster. From the south take I-71 north to US 30 east. Exit SR 3 south but turn north (right) and then left on Liberty which will become Mechanicsburg Road. Follow the gravel road on your left at 4300 Mechanicsburg Road down past the house to the open barn. Trailhead and map is at the barn. Coming from Cleveland you will likely take I-71 south to SR 3 or SR 83 south. Turn right (west) on Smithville Western Road and left (south) on Mechanicsburg Road.

Notes: This is a private property Pay-To-Ride trail. Currently $3/day. Quoting Dr. Knob, "We're not for everyone, so pay after you ride if you enjoyed yourself." Three bucks is a bargain so don't be afraid to tip even more. Trails open daily May 1 through October 31. Weekends only November 1 through April 30. Killbuck Run closed October 1 through Memorial Day. Closed during deer gun season. If you don't like the rules then go ride somewhere else. Information @ 330-264-7636 or www.vulturesknob.com. Emergency @ 911.

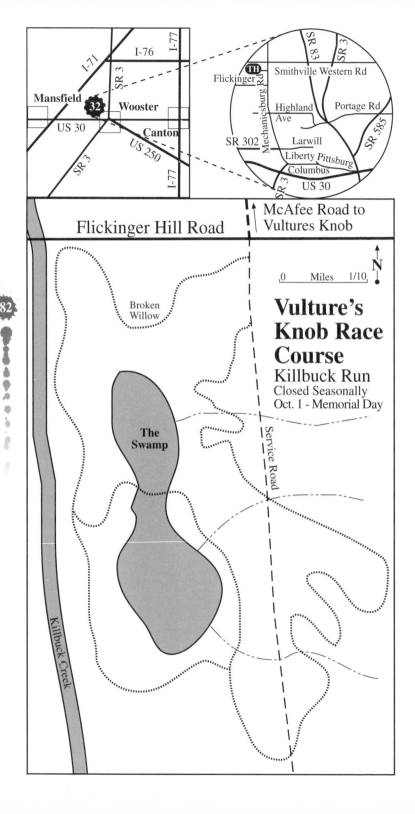

Mansfield
Wooster
Canton

I-71
I-76
I-77
SR 3
US 30
SR 3
US 250
I-77

32

SR 83
SR 3
TH
Flickinger
Smithville Western Rd
Highland Ave
Portage Rd
SR 585
SR 302
Larwill
Liberty
Pittsburg
Columbus
US 30
SR 3
Mechanicsburg Rd

Flickinger Hill Road

↑ McAfee Road to
Vultures Knob

N

0   Miles   1/10

Broken
Willow

**Vulture's
Knob Race
Course**
Killbuck Run
Closed Seasonally
Oct. 1 - Memorial Day

**The
Swamp**

Service Road

Killbuck Creek

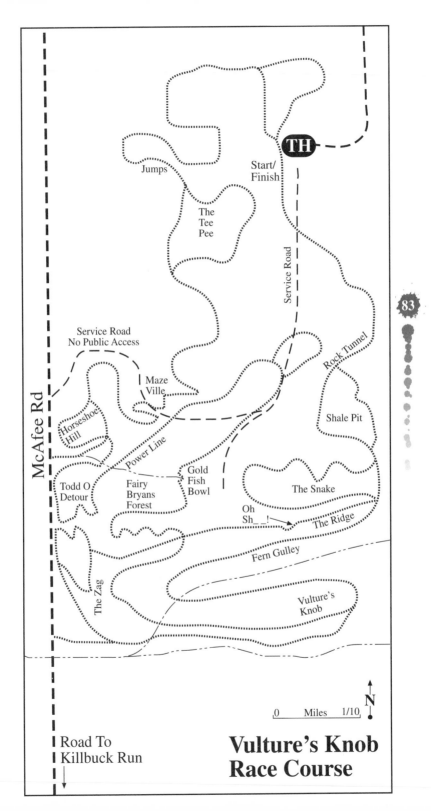

McAfee Rd

Jumps

Start/
Finish

TH

The
Tee
Pee

Service Road

83

Rock Tunnel

Service Road
No Public Access

Maze
Ville

Horseshoe
Hill

Power Line

Shale Pit

Todd O
Detour

Fairy
Bryans
Forest

Gold
Fish
Bowl

The Snake

Oh
Sh__!

The Ridge

Fern Gulley

The Zag

Vulture's
Knob

0   Miles   1/10

N

Road To
Killbuck Run

Vulture's Knob
Race Course

Quail Hollow State Park

2 miles / Easy

Overview: This trail was established by NOMBA and is some of the only legal singletrack close to Cleveland. A short 2 mile trail rolls through hardwoods, pines, open fields and poison ivy. Yep, another section of prime real estate given to mountain bikers. You might want to wear long sleeves to avoid the itch. Good beginner ride.

Trail Description: This point-to-point trail starts south of the main park road. Singletrack winds it way though a pine forest, then hardwoods, before entering open meadows. The last half mile runs back into dense woods and ends at Duquette Avenue. This is a pretty level trail and a good spot for that family ride. To make it interesting there are a few logs to hop, while bridges span the wetter areas. And this place can get wet. It is one of the only parks in Ohio to have seasonal trail closures when it's just too sloppy to ride. Though occasionally inconvenient for riders, kudos to the park management. Other state parks could learn a lesson here. At Duquette you can road ride 2.5 miles back to the entrance or put in 2 more miles on the trail. Hey, that's why you're here, right?

How To Get There: From the north follow I-77 south through Akron. Past Akron you want to get on SR 619. You cannot exit directly from I-77 to SR 619. Look for the Arlington Road exit. Follow this south to SR 619. Turn left and follow SR 619 east to Hartville. Turn left on Prospect Avenue and follow the signs into the park.

Notes: Good local resource but needs more trail to make it worth a rode trip. Trail Maintenance by NOMBA. Park @ 330-877-6652. Emergency @ 911.

84

The "Dueling Logs" at Vulture's Knob.

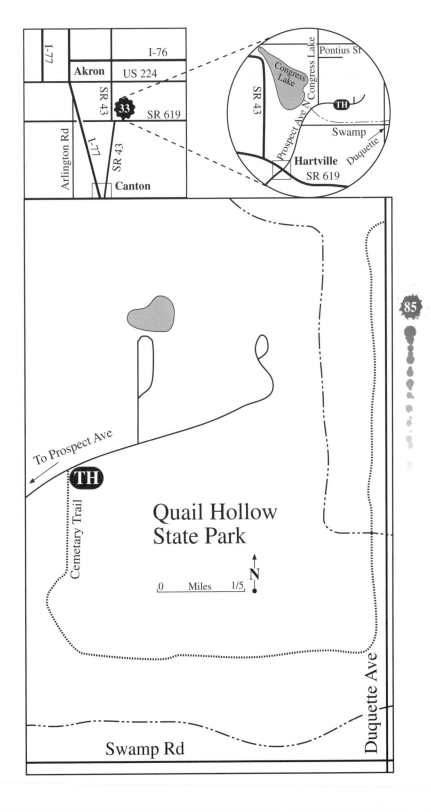

I-1

I-76

Akron US 224

SR 43

33 SR 619

Arlington Rd

I-77

SR 43

Canton

Pontius St

Congress Lake

SR 43

Prospect Ave N

Congress Lake

TH

Swamp

Duquette

Hartville
SR 619

To Prospect Ave

TH

Cemetary Trail

Quail Hollow
State Park

N

0   Miles   1/5

85

Duquette Ave

Swamp Rd

Findley State Park

2 miles / Easy

Overview: These trails follow the small rolling hills bordering Findley Lake. A family oriented park, the trails reflect this in their wide open nature which anyone can ride and enjoy. Yet another park where you can load up the kid's bikes and not worry if it will be too difficult for them to enjoy.

Trail Description: If you're camping you can start at Spillway Trail, east of the lake. This is a flat trail with some nice lakeside views along the way. The only real challenge is riding down into and out of the overflow spillway. No, there's no water in it. The kids will get a kick out of this and probably want to do it again. After crossing the dam take a left toward the beach. Past the beach choose either Black Locust or Larch Trail. Larch trail will cross Park Road 1 and continue to the parking area. The ride totals almost 2 miles. Unfortunately, the trail doesn't continue south of the lake, so you must either turn around or road ride back on Park Road 3. Watch out for traffic if you road ride back. Hopefully, the park will open the Buckeye Trail to bikes, like Scioto Trail State Park did successfully, and complete the loop around the lake.

How To Get There: From Cleveland take I-71 south past I-271. Take the next exit, SR 18, west. Follow SR 18 through Medina to Wellington. In Wellington go left on SR 58. The park entrance is about 3 miles south on the left. From the south take I-71 north to US 250 west. Follow US 250 into Ashland. In Ashland turn right on SR 58 north. Follow SR 58 past US 224 to the park entrance on the right.

Notes: Park @ 440-647-4490. Emergency @ 911.

A view from Lakeside Trail at Jefferson Lake State Park.

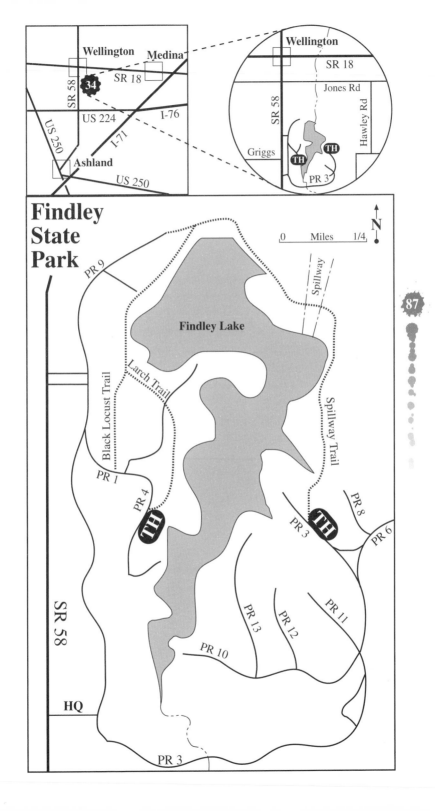

Wellington Medina

SR 58

SR 18

34

US 224

I-76

US 250

I-71

Ashland

US 250

Wellington

SR 18

Jones Rd

SR 58

Hawley Rd

Griggs

TH

TH

PR 3

Findley State Park

PR 9

0 Miles 1/4

N

Findley Lake

Spillway

Larch Trail

Black Locust Trail

Spillway Trail

PR 1

PR 4

TH

PR 3

TH

PR 8

PR 6

SR 58

PR 13

PR 12

PR 11

PR 10

HQ

PR 3

87

Alpine Valley Ski Resort

3 miles / Moderate

Overview: The is the first Ohio ski resort to follow the national trend and open its slopes to mountain bikes in the off-season on a pay-to-ride basis. It's a natural partnership - they have mountains, we have bikes. For riders in the Cleveland area this ride is practically within the city limits. You know what this means - no more illegal night rides in the metroparks! Alpine Valley originally opened its trails for racing and has since expanded to weekly seasonal use.

Trail Description: Just what should you expect from your ride? One mother of a hill. Unfortunately, that's about it. Just one. Granted, it's a big hill, which 3 miles of trail carve up, over, and around creating a moderately intense singletrack loop. In between races you have a variety of options which will take you through a fast, rocky course. Locals lament the loss of trails on the back of the ski hill to development, as urban sprawl moves in a nightmare-ish "It Came from Cleveland" B-movie. The terrain can be muddy, or bone dry and dusty. And there are the ever present, grassy green ski slopes for your amusement. Looking downhill with the useless ski lifts above, you will definitely feel the need for speed. In the winter you can participate in a snow slalom - just like the X-games. Sorta. This is the best thing going in Cleveland. Then again, it's the only thing going in Cleveland.

How To Get There: From Cleveland take I-271 north to US 322 east (Mayfield Rd). Alpine Valley will be on your left four miles east of SR 306 on SR 322, 10620 Mayfield Rd, Chesterland, Ohio.

Notes: This is a private property Pay-To-Ride trail. Currently $4/day. Open May through October, Wednesdays 4:00pm until dusk and Sundays 12:00 until dusk. Closed all other days. Helmet required and you must sign a waiver. If you don't like the rules then go ride somewhere else. Office @ 440-285-2211 or Snowline @ 440-729-9775. Emergency @ 911.

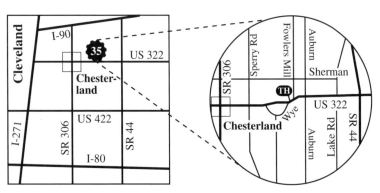

Atchinson

3 miles / Moderate

Overview: Cleveland riders, someone has finally heard your prayers - Lake Metro Parks! This short ride has a little bit of everything and is a must do for anyone living in this part of the state. Expect climbs, descents, drops, logs, mud, overhanging trees and great vistas!

Trail Description: This 3 mile trail starts off tight-n-windy, then opens up a bit as it follows along the Grand River. Along the Grand River Valley you will be treated to one of the best scenic views northeast Ohio has to offer. Riding the trail counter-clockwise it first follows, then descends down into, the valley on a route technical riders will appreciate. Enjoy your view of the river then start your climb out. The remainder of the trail winds its way through the upland woods and makes good use of a small space with creative loops. Most of these are fast and twisting with lots of logs to hop. Let's hope they are able to build more smart trail, and that Cleveland Metro Parks takes a look at what can be done by working together with bikers. Lastly, the park is bordered by private property, so don't stray.

How To Get There: From Cleveland take I-90 east to SR 528. Turn south on SR 528. To find the trailhead go left onto SR 307 east. Follow SR 307 east for about a mile. Just past Bates Road begin looking for the Lake Metro Parks sign on the right. *Do not* park at the trailhead. Instead, park at Riverview Park and road ride to the trailhead. To find Riverview Park take a right on Bates Road then a left on Bailey.

Notes: If you enjoyed your ride here you should join NOMBA. It's that simple. Lake Metro Parks @ 444-358-7275. Emergency @ 911.

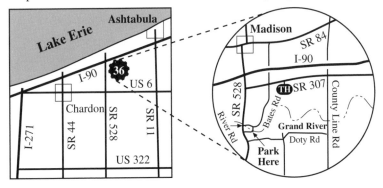

Ohio Mountain Biking Organizations

Central Ohio Mountain Bike Organization (COMBO)
Promoting responsible mountain biking in Central Ohio through trail building, maintenance, and group rides.
5500 Emerson Ave.
Worthington, OH 43085
614-847-4396

Northeast Ohio Mountain Bike Association (NOMBA)
Promoting mountain bicycling opportunities through environmentally and socially responsible land use.
890 Iroquois Run
Macedonia, Ohio 44056
330-467-4751

Queen City Wheels of Greater Cincinnati (QCW)
Promotes sanctioned bicycle racing throughout the Greater Cincinnati area, advocates cycling awareness with local governments, and provides members with coaching and camaraderie.
185 Albright Dr.
Loveland, OH 45140
513-677-7356

The Dayton Cycling Club (DCC)
Dedicated to the promotion of all aspects of bicycling. Everyone who is interested in bicycling - whether for health, recreation, competition, transportation or fellowship - is welcome to join.
P.O. Box 94, Wright Brothers Branch
Dayton, OH 45409

The Cincinnati Cycle Club (CCC)
Promotes bicycling for sport, recreation, health, friendship, and we work to improve bicycling safety and facilities.
P.O. Box 800
Milford, OH 45150
513-791-7190

Lake Erie Wheelers
We are interested in all facets of cycling: touring, recreation, fitness, mountain biking, and racing.
P.O. Box 770744
Lakewood, OH 44107
440-779-2533

Ohio Bicycle Federation (OBF)
The OBF is an alliance of individuals and organizations interested in promoting the use of bicycles for recreation, transportation and other appropriate purposes.
40 W. Forth St.
Dayton, Ohio 45402-1827

National Mountain Biking Organizations

International Mountain Biking Association (IMBA)
The mission of IMBA is to promote mountain bicycling opportunities that are environmentally and socially responsible.
P.O. Box 7578
Boulder, CO 80306
303-545-9011

IMBA Ohio State Representative
James Buratti
1730 North Star Drive #7
Columbus, OH 43212
614-486-2684

National Off-Road Bicycle Association (NORBA)
NORBA's mission is to guide, service and promote mountain biking as a competitive sport and outdoor activity.
One Olympic Plaza
Colorado Springs, CO 80909
719-578-4717

The trailhead never looked so good.
Until next time...

About the author: James Buratti has been mountain biking in Ohio for the past six years. Possessing a Masters in Natural Resources, he believes that mountain biking does not have to be ecologically destructive. Well planned and maintained trails, combined with thoughtful and involved riders, can assure an environmentally sound sport. James is the Ohio State Representative for the International Mountain Bicycling Association and former president of the Central Ohio Mountain Bike Organization. He urges everyone who rides, whether for recreation or competition, to volunteer for trail maintenance on your local trail. If no trail days are organized, start one yourself. You owe it to the sport and you owe it to the land.

James Buratti

Essential Mountain Biking Lingo

Brain Bucket/Skid Lid/Your Protection: A helmet.

Endo: An abrupt stop which sends the rider flying over their handlebars. Short for end-over-end. "The creek was deeper than she though and she did an endo right into it."

Doubletrack: A piece of trail wide enough for two bikes to ride side by side, usually an old road.

Full Suspension: A mountain bike with both front and rear suspension.

Hardtail: A mountain bike with front suspension and no rear suspension.

Hike-A-Bike: When you and your bike go for a walk. Usually up a steep hill but could also be a very technical section or wandering lost through the woods. "I had to hike-a-bike up that huge hill."

Off-camber: A trail which is sloping at two separate angles, such as downhill and also to the side. Makes for technical riding. "I started out okay but lost all traction on the off-camber section."

ORV/APV: Off Road Vehicle/All Purpose Vehicle. Motorized two and four wheeled vehicles and their drivers. Found throughout Ohio.

Rigid: A bike with no suspension, either front or rear.

Scooby Do: The flailing of ones feet in a mid-air pedaling motion while going nowhere; occurs after you've already lost contact with the pedals. Often followed by an endo. "His front tire planted that log and he just Scooby-Dood for a minute."

Singletrack: A piece of trail wide enough for only one bike to travel on.

Sonny Bono: Plowing head-first into a tree or other solid object. "She almost pulled a Sonny Bono when she missed the turn."

Schwag: Free bike stuff given out at races, trails days, and other cycling events.

The Pee-Pee Dance: An unplanned dismount where you straddle the top tube with one leg on each side while trying not to rack yourself or fall over. (Picture a small child that needs to pee. Ah ha, you say!) Often occurs in failed climbs while hopping backwards downhill. "Chris blew it right at the top of the climb then did The Pee-Pee Dance half way down."

IMBA Rules of The Trail

1. Ride on open trails only

2. Leave no trace

3. Control your bicycle

4. Always yield trail

5. Never spook animals

6. Plan ahead

Mountain Biking Ohio
Order Form

Quantity	Title	Cost	Total
_____	Mountain Biking Ohio A Guide to Singletrack Trails in the Buckeye State	$11.95	$_____
	Shipping & Handling		$ 3.00
	Total Payment		$_____

Name _____

Shipping _____
Address _____

Mail to:
Single Track Press
1730 North Star Rd. #7
Columbus OH 43212

Don't forget to include a check or money order.
Allow two weeks for delivery.

<u>Notes</u>

Notes